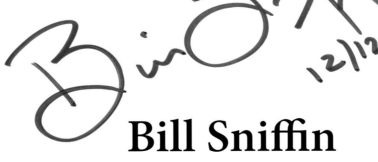

To Dave Saliga

Enjoy Wyoming!

Bill Sniffin
12/12

Wyoming's
7 Greatest Natural Wonders
+ 33 Other Fascinating Places

Bill Sniffin

with contributing photographers & writers

PUBLISHED BY MOUNTAIN AMERICA, INCORPORATED

(A DIVISION OF WCS CORPORATION)

Previous page: Pioneer photographer Dean Conger snapped this image of the Lower Falls in Yellowstone Canyon with a fisheye lens 40 years ago. He recalls that the viewfinder fell off the camera to the bottom of the canyon during the shot.

Above: Three eagles on the North Fork of the Shoshone River near Cody seemed engrossed in conversation when J. L. Woody Wooden captured this image.

WYOMING'S 7 GREATEST NATURAL WONDERS + 33 OTHER FASCINATING PLACES

For information, contact
Mountain America, Incorporated
P.O. Box 900
Lander, WY 82520
USA

First edition published in 2012 by Mountain America, Incorporated, a division of WCS Corporation. Printed in China.

www.billsniffin.com

IBSN 9780-9639350-4-5

For Library of Congress Cataloging in Publication Data, contact the publisher at the address above.

WELCOME TO OUR WYOMING

by Matthew H. Mead, Governor of Wyoming

If you are reading this, you are already hooked on this book—and rightly so. It is a book with a unique perspective on the Great State of Wyoming—one to peruse again and again.

Bill Sniffin is a well-known Wyoming newspaper columnist. He has received acclaim far and wide for his work. In this newest book, Bill takes a fresh look at our state and because he knows Wyoming so well, you will want to see what he found.

The book had its origins in one of Bill's most popular columns, written a few years ago, about Wyoming's 7 Greatest Natural Wonders. With a little help from his friends and readers, Bill chose 33 other wonderful places in Wyoming to showcase, too, and this book is the result.

Featured within are stunning photographs and wonderful write-ups about many of Wyoming's most beautiful locations. More than 30 of the best photographers in the state were involved with this project and they had great material to work with: Wyoming in all its glory. So, here you have page after page of Wyoming at its best in photographs and stories.

This is a collection of images and information that reminds us of the many wonders located throughout Wyoming. It inspires us to think about the natural beauty that abounds. It inspires us to plan our next visits to these special spots.

Congratulations to Bill and to all the photographers and writers for producing such a fine tribute to Wyoming.

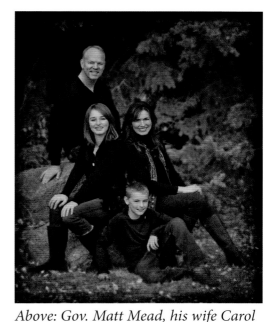

Above: Gov. Matt Mead, his wife Carol and children Pete and Mary.

Below: Shoshone Lake and the Wind River Mountains are visible from the top of Cyclone Pass, by Bill Sniffin.

A SHOWCASE OF WONDERS AND GREAT PHOTOGRAPHERS

You are holding in your hands a true labor of love. It is a project a half decade in the making. It has involved the author, seven other writers (including a U. S. Senator), a governor and 30 other photographers plus designers, printers, distributors and other helpers. Whew! Sure glad to finally celebrate the birth, after a prolonged labor and oft-times difficult delivery.

By my count, it has been at least five years since a photo-oriented book about Wyoming has been published. That was by Fred Plughoft of Pinedale, one of our photographers featured here.

Sometimes it is amazing to see the transformation between what you start out trying to create and what you end up with at the end of the process. In the case of this book, it was going to include some of my columns and a selection of my favorite color slides from 42 years of living in Wyoming. I had invited Scott Copeland of Lander and Lander native Randy Wagner to submit photos to fill out the book.

Scott and Randy still have the majority of photos in the book. But we have added 28 other photographers!

Who are these incredible men and women?

Below: Titcomb Basin deep in the Wind River Mountains outside of Lander, captured by Scott Copeland.

Above: Author Bill Sniffin paused during photographing the Firehole Canyon area of the Green River north of Flaming Gorge when Jim Smail took this photo.

Below: Smoke from a distant fire contributed to this unusual cloud formation and subsequent solar rays during a sunset in Lander by Bill Sniffin.

Where did they come from? Have I been living under a rock?

We know that Wyoming has fantastic vistas. Seven million tourists a year attest to that. But did we know that these men and women are sacrificing their lives, their livelihoods and their precious family time to stalk these amazing Wyoming scenes? They have snapped images that have completely blown me away. They will blow you away, too.

Be sure to thank them if you see them.

When you start from scratch on a project, you can make it as unique as possible. And we did do that.

Among the unique things in this book are 14 foldouts, much like a larger version of *National Geographic* magazine. I wanted this book to showcase Wyoming's photographers and Wyoming's fascinating places like no other book before.

The book is inspired by and carries the same title as a column that I wrote in 2007 concerning picking out the state's greatest natural wonders. That column can be found on the next page.

Thus, the book is divided into the 7 sections, each one centered on a natural "wonder." We added photos from the same parts of the state to the end pages of the various sections.

We were super lucky to have Wagner, Shelli Johnson, Clay James, Jim Smail, Sen. Mike Enzi, Gene Bryan and Pat Schmidt to write about our 7 wonders. Gov. Matt Mead got involved by writing a very nice welcome. If you see these folks, be sure to thank them. They met some unreal deadlines and put their hearts and souls into their writings.

I learned a lot from what they wrote and you will, too. If you bought this book you already love Wyoming. And you will know that these seven writers (+ 31 photographers) love Wyoming, too.

—Bill Sniffin

Wyoming's 7 Greatest Natural Wonders

One of the things that the Wyoming Travel and Tourism Division attempts to sell to tourists is how "natural" our state is.

It was with that goal in mind that I decided not long ago to try to determine the most impressive seven natural wonders of our state.

When the idea came to me to promote what seemed the most likely seven wonders, well, it was not as easy as originally thought.

With lots of friends around the state, I made the mistake of asking them what areas they thought would qualify.

**by
Bill Sniffin**

They came up with at least 50 wonders. You can bet when this column gets published from one end of the state to the other, well, my readers will let me know what an incomplete list it is. Doggone it, why isn't my favorite place listed?

Two wonders were on everybody's list.

NUMBER ONE was Yellowstone National Park, the world's first national park. And what a wonder it is!

NUMBER TWO was its next-door neighbor, the Grand Tetons/Jackson Hole area.

NUMBER THREE, most also agreed, should be the world's first national monument, Devils Tower, along with the Wyoming Black Hills, which it dominates.

But coming up with the four other wonders proved to be somewhat more controversial.

Kari Cooper of Jackson says the most beautiful place in Wyoming is the headwaters of the Green River near Pinedale. Carole Perkins of Sheridan touted Shell Falls outside of Greybull.

Former Cheyenne resident Mike Lindsey could not imagine how the Oregon Trail could not make the list. State Rep. Pete Illoway of Cheyenne pushed hard for Hell's Half Acre and Wind River Canyon, with the latter also being Tucker Fagan's favorite.

Former Gov. Mike Sullivan, of Casper, pitched the Chugwater formation, with its red rocks ranging from Flaming Gorge to Red Canyon to Thermopolis.

Rodger McDaniel of Cheyenne said he thought Elk Mountain, Gannett Peak and any one of several rivers should be on my list. Secretary of State Max Maxfield likes the Big Horn Mountains and also boosted Sinks Canyon.

Former *Rawlins Daily Times* publisher Shelley Ridenour talked about Aspen Alley on the Battle Mountain Highway and Silver Lake in the Snowy Range. Former publisher Pat Schmidt of the *Thermopolis Independent Record* lobbied for the Beartooth Mountains.

Worland State Rep. Debbie Hammons said that surely my list would include The Medicine Wheel and Chief Joseph Highway.

Retired bed and breakfast owner Marv Brown lobbied hard for Devils Gate and Red Canyon.

Tom Lacock, formerly of Cheyenne, wanted Wind River Canyon and the Saratoga Hot Springs included.

Pennie Hunt of Laramie thought our wide-open spaces should be listed. The Great Divide Basin in the Red Desert was pushed by Charlie Smith.

Dave Langerman wanted more waterfalls. Vince Tomassi of Diamondville railed at me for not touting Fossil Butte. My daughter Shelli Johnson thought Bighorn Canyon deserved consideration.

Jeff Rose of Lingle likes Guernsey State Park and Vedauwoo, outside of Laramie.

Jim Hicks of Buffalo said the Seven Brothers Lakes and Lake Solitude are four-mile hikes into the Cloud Peak Wilderness and deserve consideration. Ernie Over pushed for Togwotee Pass and the red walls around Butch Cassidy country.

Former Travel Commission Director Gene Bryan offered a host of sites including the usual suspects but also added the gangplank west of Cheyenne, Wapiti Valley, McCullough Peaks, Greybull's Sheep Mountain and a special plug for South Pass for what it meant to the country.

NUMBER FOUR, many agreed, should be the vast Red Desert, with all its various sites including the many buttes, Boars Tusk, Killpecker Sand Dunes and all the other unique places tucked away in this gigantic area.

NUMBER FIVE became obvious. Because Thermopolis Hot Springs is the largest in the world it was easy to include.

Whew. Just two left to go.

NUMBER SIX? Rodger is right. I need to include at least one river on my list. My choice is the North Platte River system. This huge river makes up five reservoirs and carries more water than any other river in our state.

But we sure have wonderful rivers like the Snake, Green, Laramie, Sweetwater, Popo Agie, Wind/Bighorn, Greybull, Tongue and even the Powder. But the North Platte is number six on my list, with all its wondrous sites from Saratoga to Casper to Torrington.

NUMBER SEVEN is South Pass, with all its meaning to the country. Without this natural gap in the mountain ranges, the USA of today would probably only reach to the mountains. Some 350,000 emigrants traveled the Oregon, California and Mormon Trails in the 19th century over South Pass to extend our country to the Pacific. The history around that area is superb for any tourist to enjoy.

So there you have it.

No doubt you will not agree on all of them. You should agree with me that there are hundreds of places that are wonderful natural wonders to see in our great state.

What are your 7 favorite natural wonders of Wyoming?

This column was first published in 2007.

Left: A hiker is silhouetted against the volcanic pillar called "God's Rod" on Black Mountain west of Cody. The Buffalo Bill Reservoir with Cedar and Rattlesnake Mountains are visible in the distance. Photo by Dewey Vanderhoff.

Table of Contents

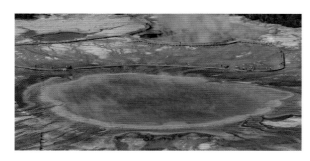

My Yellowstone Park: 8-33

My Teton Park: 34-53

My South Pass: 54-71

My North Platte
River: 72-89

My Devils Tower: 90-107

My Red Desert: 108-129

My Thermopolis: 130-155

MY YELLOWSTONE PARK

Over the years, the park became my favorite place

by Shelli Johnson

When I was three, my parents moved us from Harlan, Iowa, to Lander, Wyoming. Nothing against Iowa, but I consider the move one of the greatest gifts from my parents. My backyard includes the Wind River Mountains and Yellowstone.

During my childhood, we experienced many weekends in the world's first national park. We'd load the car with a tank of gas, ourselves, the makings for a picnic, and head to Yellowstone. We played tourists, often touring the Grand Loop Road and stopping at all the main overlooks and geyser basins to get a closer look at the sights.

Yellowstone is home to the world's largest collection of geysers. One of my earliest memories of Yellowstone is watching Old Faithful erupt. I remember thinking there was a person in a closet somewhere nearby turning on the geyser at regular intervals. Even though I have watched Old Faithful erupt countless times, I continue to be amazed by the experience. The spouting water shows, hissing vents and colorful pools that smelled like rotten eggs were mysterious wonders to me then—and now.

Over the years, Yellowstone became my favorite place.

In 1992, my husband, Jerry, and I spent part of our honeymoon in Yellowstone. After checking into our room at the historic Lake Yellowstone Hotel, I was in the bathroom getting freshened up when I noticed several people looking through our window from a short distance, with cameras and binoculars. I was flattered, but Jerry had a different reaction, so he went outside, only to discover there was a bull moose right outside our bathroom window that visitors were viewing.

The historic Lake Hotel's lobby is an amazing place. The lobby is elegant and overlooks the beautiful Yellowstone Lake, which covers 136 square miles, and is the largest freshwater lake situated above 7,000 feet in North America. During summer evenings, there is often a string quartet or piano player performing in the lobby.

In 1994, we moved to Gardiner, MT, to start Yellowstone Journal Corporation. I'll never forget the first interview I had scheduled for our newspaper, *Yellowstone Journal*. I was to meet with the late great Rick Hutchinson, Yellowstone's geyser expert. A little nervous about my first official assignment, I headed out of the house to get an early start for the 5-mile drive to Mammoth Hot Springs. But I wasn't going anywhere. A lazy bull bison lay directly behind our truck, preventing me from going anywhere. That was my first lesson from the world's first national park: Yellowstone, like other natural wonders, is on its own schedule.

Over the course of 15 years, we operated and expanded Yellowstone Journal Corporation before selling the business to Active Interest Media, owner of *Backpacker, Yoga Journal, Climbing,* and other magazines, in September 2008.

We worked very hard at the business and made sacrifices along the way, but mostly it was upside. The greatest benefit was the opportunity to experience Yellowstone and its wonders on an almost-constant basis. (While operating the Yellowstone Journal business, we logged probably no fewer than 200 visits to Yellowstone.)

Today Jerry and I have three sons, Wolf, 12, Hayden, 10, and Finis, 5. Wolf was named after our favorite animal, which since 1995, has been making a remarkable comeback in Yellowstone and the surrounding region. Hayden is named for Ferdinand Hayden, geologist and pioneering surveyor who led the first official survey of Yellowstone in 1871, and for which Hayden Valley is named. Before Yellowstone became a national park, Hayden was Yellowstone's most enthusiastic advocate. (Finis gets his name from the late Finis Mitchell, who was a famous and important explorer of our backyard, Wyoming's Wind River Range.)

Now, we are the parents taking our children to Yellowstone.

Most people don't realize it, but 98 percent of the park is considered backcountry. If, when you visit Yellowstone, you remain mostly in your car and limit your visit to some of the boardwalk hikes and overlooks, you're only seeing a tiny sliver of Yellowstone. Despite its 3 million visitors per year, it is not that difficult to wander off the beaten path—just a little—and feel like you have the place all to yourself.

I remember interviewing Lee Whittlesey, Yellowstone's historical archivist, and author of several Yellowstone books, about the park's early visitors. He explained that because the park's early visitors arrived on horse, and in stagecoaches, their travel was slow, causing them to see more than today's visitors see. That remark has stuck with me and in fact, caused me to approach our own Yellowstone visits in a different way.

We can visit a place or we can experience it. Since that interview, I have aimed to experience Yellowstone rather than

Opposite: A classic image of the Lower Falls of the Yellowstone River in the Grand Canyon of the park by Daryl Hunter.

visit it. Instead of trying to see it all in a single trip, we now choose a particular area (Northern Range or Canyon or Lower Loop?) or a particular feature (geysers, grand vistas or wildlife?) and explore Yellowstone more intimately. We are lucky because Yellowstone is just 3 hours from where we live, so we can return often.

As a result of our many experiences I have some recommendations for others looking to experience the world's first national park.

Sights:

Lamar Valley is an extraordinary place. The scenery and diversity of wildlife one can see make it so. The entire Northern Range, for that matter, is so spectacular that even if you just drive through it, slowly taking in the sights from the car, it is nothing short of an amazing scenic drive.

I have a particular soft spot for the Grand Canyon of the Yellowstone, a 23-mile-long canyon that stretches from Upper Falls to Tower Fall. The colorful canyon is 1,500 to 4,000 feet across, and 800 to 1,200 feet deep.

I have been to this region of Yellowstone too many times to count. Every single visit, upon looking into—and across—this grand abyss, it is as if it's my first. I can be moved to tears by its beauty. The canyon includes the 308-foot-tall Lower Falls and the 109-foot-tall Upper Falls. It is truly a sight to behold.

One of my family's favorite ways to experience the Grand Canyon of the Yellowstone is to view the Lower Falls from afar, up close, and near its brink. We do this by stopping first at Artist Point overlook, where one can enjoy a distant-but-glorious view of Lower Falls. Usually we have a picnic lunch near this overlook.

Then, we become more acquainted with the Lower Falls by hiking Uncle Tom's Trail. The hike is only one mile roundtrip and involves descending a couple of switchbacks, followed by 500 metal steps, to the base of the Lower Falls. Often there is a rainbow cutting through the voluminous waterfall, and on hot days its mist provides relief. Unfortunately, what goes down must go up, which in this case is a metal staircase containing 500 steps. For what it's worth, the return hike is one of the most scenic natural stair-climbers I've ever been on (and I've been on many).

To cap our Canyon experience, we love hiking to the brink of the Lower Falls. This hike is one mile, roundtrip, and will take you right to the top of Lower Falls. You'll be able to look right over its brink as it dumps huge amounts of water into a dark green pool in the canyon below.

I have a unique memory from this hike that I can't resist sharing. Our son, Hayden, 3, was in a backpack on Jerry, and our oldest son, Wolf, 5, ran a little ahead of us as we hiked on the Lower Falls Brink trail. I didn't want him to get too far ahead of us, so I yelled, "Wolf!", not once but a couple of times. Visitors all around us stopped in their tracks and got their binoculars out, hoping to see a wolf on the trail. They did, but it wasn't of the wild canid variety.

Driving from Canyon over Dunraven Pass to Tower Fall is another outstanding way to experience Yellowstone's astounding scenery. A favorite hike is Mount Washburn, which starts from the top of Dunraven Pass. This is a 5.5-mile or 6-mile roundtrip hike, depending on if you start at Chittenden parking area or Dunraven Pass picnic area. In my humble opinion, no other hike in Yellowstone provides such a panoramic view. The hike, which dishes out about 1,400' of elevation gain, is a little bit of work, but well worth it. Once at the 10,243-foot-tall summit, the views include most of northern Yellowstone, and on a clear day, a glimpse of Wyoming's Teton Range.

The Tower/Roosevelt to Mammoth Hot Springs route is one of the most scenic drives available and visitors can see a variety of interesting sights, and will likely spy some wild animals, too. At Mammoth Hot Springs, you can often see elk, and hike a few trails that are easily accessed and provide visitors with close-up views of Minerva Terrace.

Yellowstone Lake, as mentioned earlier, is stunning. I recommend indulging in an ice cream treat from the Yellowstone General Store while walking along the shore of the vast, high mountain lake.

Hayden Valley is a large, sub-alpine valley located between Yellowstone Lake and the Grand Canyon of the Yellowstone. It is not only a beautiful expanse of country, but a great place from which to view wildlife.

Wild Animals:

Yellowstone is a wild place. Hundreds of species of mammals, birds, fish and reptiles have been documented in Yellowstone, including several that are either endangered or threatened. Yellowstone Park is home to the most famous megafauna (large or "charismatic") wild animals in the Lower 48 states.

Grizzly bears, black bears, wolves, elk, bison, moose, pronghorn, deer, bighorn sheep, mountain lions, plus many other wild animals, large and small, live in Yellowstone.

Yellowstone's bison are truly famous. The bison herd, about 3,700-strong, is the last remaining free-ranging herd in the United States. The bison that Yellowstone visitors see are descended from a remnant population of a mere 23 animals that survived the massive slaughter of the 25-60 million bison that once roamed the American Plains in the 19th century.

We camp and hike a lot. Doing so in Yellowstone is wilder than doing so in our southern Wind River Range back yard. Why? Because there are grizzly bears. It just feels more wild due to this great animal's presence. It is recommended that Yellowstone visitors get informed about bear precaution protocols, especially those surrounding proper food storage and taking along bear spray when exploring in grizzly bear country.

One time Jerry I reserved a backcountry camping permit in Yellowstone's Pebble Creek region. This area provides particularly good habitat for grizzly bears. So as we camped that evening we felt presence of the grizzly. Like a dummy, the

Below: This image of Old Faithful at night, framed by the Big Dipper, took 40 seconds of time exposure by Dewey Vanderhoff in 1982. The glow off the geyser is from the light of a full October moon.

book I brought to read in the tent was *Bear Attacks,* by Stephen Herrero. That night, every time we heard a twig snap we were certain a grizzly was coming to get us. Hiking in a place that is as wild as Yellowstone—home to grizzly bears, wolves and other large wild animals—absolutely provides a special experience. You can feel the presence of these animals when you hike even if you never see them.

The comeback of wolves in Yellowstone is an amazing story. As owner of *Yellowstone Journal,* I had the great honor of accompanying Yellowstone's various experts in the field. My most unforgettable was a day spent with Wolf Project leader Doug Smith. It was early April, at the end of the the project's winter study, and Doug invited me to shadow him and his team. Hearing a wolf howl for the first time in Yellowstone is an experience I will never forget. Looking into a black wolf's golden eyes through one of Doug's scopes that morning remains a vivid memory. By noon, I had viewed 21 wolves. It was an unbelievable experience.

On another occasion I got to accompany the Yellowstone's then-ornithologist Terry McEneaney. After doing some bird counts, we stopped in Hayden Valley and watched from a close-but-safe distance as a grizzly bear, fresh out of hibernation, plucked pocket gophers from the ground and ate them

whole. We were so close I could see the red in the grizzly's eyes through Terry's scope.

Great places to view wildlife include Hayden and Lamar valleys, and the entire Northern Range. Bison and elk and moose can sometimes be seen near the geyser basins and Yellowstone Lake. The best time to view wildlife is during early morning or evening hours, preferably in spring, early summer, or fall. Wildlife may also be viewed during peak summer season, just not in great numbers because animals are often inhabiting higher elevations.

GEYSERS:

As for geysers, our favorites are the following.

A Yellowstone experience is not complete without seeing Old Faithful erupt. This geyser is in the Upper Geyser Basin and erupts every 60-90 minutes. It's quite a show. Beehive Geyser, located near Old Faithful, is another favorite geyser to watch erupt. While in the Old Faithful area, I urge you to stop in at the historic Old Faithful Inn, designed by architect Robert Reamer, and completed in 1904. Stroll around inside the lobby, and you'll step back in time and feel as if you're one of the Park's early visitors. It is a great experience.

In Midway Geyser Basin, take the short walk to see Grand Prismatic Spring, a huge and colorful hot spring that is the third largest natural hot spring in the world. While in the Midway Geyser Basin area, consider one of our favorite hikes, Fairy Falls. The trailhead for this hike, which takes you to the 200-foot-high dazzling Fairy Falls, can be found one mile south of Midway Geyser Basin at a steel bridge that crosses the Firehole River.

Lower Geyser Basin is home to another of our favorite geothermal spots, Fountain Paint Pots. Fountain Paint Pots are mud pots named for the reds, yellows and browns of the mud in this area.

Shelli Johnson is founder of Yellowstone Journal and YellowstonePark.com, a writer, speaker, consultant, and life and leadership coach. Her current business, Epic Life (www. YourEpicLife.com), combines life and leadership coaching with guided epic adventure. An outdoor enthusiast, Shelli hikes approximately 700 miles a year. She blogs about many of her adventures at HaveMediaWillTravel.com. She lives in Lander, WY, with her husband, Jerry, and their three sons.

Left: Scott Copeland captured this image of an inquisitive grizzly near Sedge Bay in Yellowstone.

Opposite, top: Elk cross the Firehole River in this photo of a "hellish" Yellowstone scene by Randy Wagner.

Opposite, bottom: Tim Doolin captures Yellowstone's lush Hayden Valley's colors.

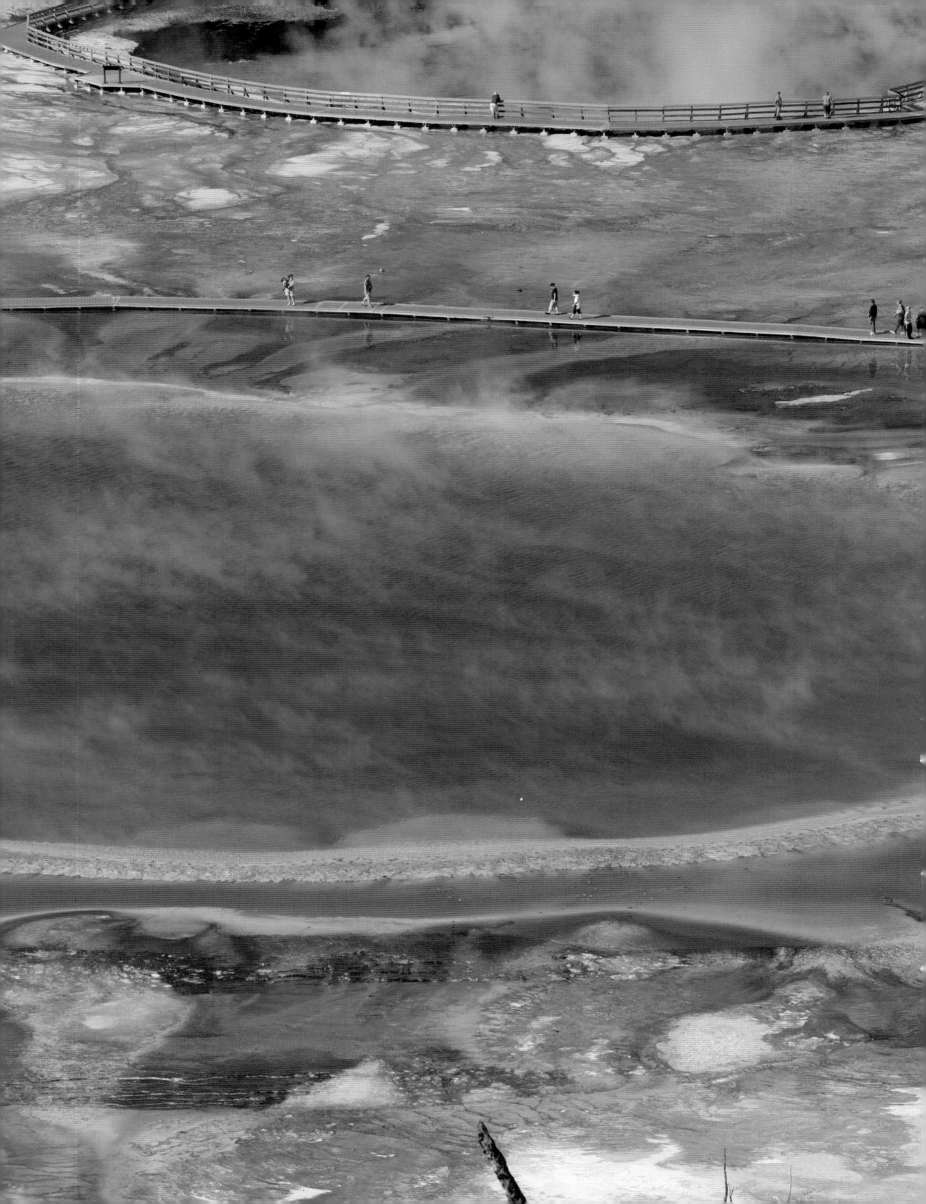

Yellowstone dazzles international visitors

By Bill Sniffin

"First, you take us to heaven. Then you take us to hell." —Uri Dan, journalist.

We in Wyoming know how wonderful Yellowstone is but the secret is out—all over the world. Today one in four visitors to the world's oldest national park, located here in our state, is from outside our country.

"Beel, do you realize how lucky you are to live near such a place?"

That question was posed to me some years ago while taking four international journalists on a tour of Yellowstone. They were in Jackson Hole attending a conference and wanted to see the park firsthand.

Heinz Tomek, head of the Austrian News Service, and Adrian Weber, a reporter from Luxembourg, sat in the front seat of the rented minivan.

Beside and behind me were two cantankerous Israeli reporters who aggressively disagreed with each other on almost everything. They were Uri Dan, a veteran reporter for the *New York Post* (who died Dec. 26, 2007 of lung cancer) and Yossi Sarid, formerly a long-time member of the Israel Knesset. Sarid is also an author and founder of an Israeli political magazine.

Yellowstone is my favorite place in the world, which qualified me as a pretty good tour guide. I am always surprised by people's reactions to the wonders of the big park. This was going to be an interesting trip.

The talkative Yossi was speechless at the beauty of the Grand Canyon of Yellowstone. It was one of those classic Wyoming fall days when the sky is a deep blue with a bright yellow sun peeking through occasional wisps of white clouds. There was very little wind, and the power of the unique waterfalls enveloped us. Yossi turned to me and said, "This is the most beautiful place I have ever seen. It is all so clear. The air so pure."

The power of the waterfall was dizzying as the water relentlessly flowed over the cliff in front of us and tumbled to the pool below.

All four men were heavy smokers and steady coffee drinkers, although they complained about how weak American coffee can be.

It was amusing to see the lunch ordered by Uri and Yossi. Both ordered a spicy dish and then poured Tabasco sauce over the chili. No ulcers for these folks. They were debating each other constantly, usually in Hebrew.

Our next stop was the Norris Geyser Basin, which is the largest such thermal area in the world. It has a science fiction feel about it as you descend into this strange area of bubbling water, steam, shooting geysers and unstable ground.

"Beel," Uri said. "One hour ago, you take us to heav-

en. Now you take us to hell! And we thought we lived in the land of the Bible." Other comments ranged from "Fellini must have designed this place." Or "so, you have your Dead Sea, too."

Uri and Yossi were both addicts of CNN. They said they can't live without it and were stunned to find a place in America without television sets. The conference was at Jackson Lake Lodge, where the cabins didn't have TVs at the time.

After three days, Uri said he was "finally getting weaned from CNN, but it is very, very difficult."

As our tour continued, I told them about Colter's Hell and the Lewis and Clark Expedition and why the park was created in the first place. And we talked about the history of the Lake Hotel and the Old Faithful Inn.

But the vast fires baffled them. They had heard about the 1988 fires but stared in disbelief at the extent of the damage still covering the forests and mountainsides. The size of the blaze was beyond their comprehension, and the stark areas of burned timber depressed them.

"How could something so awful happen in a place so beautiful?" Heinz asked. They were all familiar with the answer—that this was supposedly nature's way, but they just couldn't buy it.

While leaving the park, we spotted a big old bull elk near three cow elk. Over my objections, they jumped out of the van and ran over to the animals. They were able to get fairly close in the dense timber and watched in awe. The monarch easily moved through the closely aligned trees without hitting limbs with his antlers.

Then the bull elk started to bugle. It raised the hair on the back of my neck. What a wonderful, wilderness sound. My friends were paralyzed in their tracks. "Why is he making that strange noise?" they asked.

I wanted to answer because he was so happy to live in such a place, too, and maybe, in a way, that was true.

It might have sounded better than to just say he was wooing some girlfriends.

This newspaper column was first published in 1993.

Right: A vast amount of Yellowstone Park was burned in the famous 1988 fires. Here a bull elk stares at photographer Randy Wagner through the lines of burned trees.

Opposite, top: Castle Geyser forms spectacular images as captured by Wagner.

Opposite, bottom: Rainbows form from the water over the Lower Falls in Yellowstone Canyon. Photo by Daryl Hunter.

Previous pages:

A herd of bison makes its way along the Yellowstone River in Hayden Valley during the harsh winter as captured by Dewey Vanderhoff.

A panoramic view of the giant Grand Prismatic Spring is captured in detail by Scott Copeland.

A second panoramic photo shows Yellowstone Canyon with a full rainbow over the Lower Falls, also captured by Copeland.

Above: Lightning at sunrise over Yellowstone Lake creates unusual colors, by JL Woody Wooden.

Right: A sparkly, snowy winter scene in Yellowstone as captured by Jeff Vanuga.

Opposite: A mountain goat perches high above a wintry Sunlight Creek east of Yellowstone, by Scott Copeland.

Previous page: Mammoth Hot Springs terraces by Dan Hayward.

What about that supervolcano that lurks underneath Yellowstone?

By Bill Sniffin

So there I was, in the middle of the most beautiful place in America, and on my mind was this: what a cataclysm it would be if Yellowstone explodes!

During my annual trek to my favorite place on earth, the thought that the Yellowstone Caldera Supervolcano explodes every 600,000 years or so, and the last one was just 640,000 years ago, well, it gave me pause.

But in between those thoughts, I stopped by and said hello to Old Faithful, and she erupted right in front of me. Good timing, once again.

Inside the Old Faithful store, it was fun to chat with the clerks telling tourist stories. The gal ahead of me asked them where to buy the tickets to the geyser showing.

Earlier that day someone had asked them who manned the crew that climbed down into the geysers for the periodic cleaning of the plumbing.

A fellow Wyomingite overheard us and said he encountered some foreign tourists asking a ranger, while they were all standing along the road frozen by 100 stopped vehicles, "Are these bears wild?"

Earlier that month, they had had a power outage. Several tourists asked them if that would affect the eruptions of the geysers.

I went to the men's room, and this tall statuesque blond female was standing in line to use the sit-down toilet. Yes, she was European. The clerks said that same gal had been in a hurry when she asked them where the bathrooms were.

I was enduring and enjoying all this on Sept. 19. We old-timers can remember a time when mid-September was a barren time in the park. The only people you would see would be locals—folks from Wyoming, Montana and Idaho.

But not anymore. I think it is probably mid-October now before you can enjoy any kind of solitude during the busy times at the park's busy places. And this is just fine. Yellowstone is a wonderful place, and it is owned by all the 300,000,000 citizens of our country. It is their right to see it as much as it is mine, although I sort like to think differently most of the time.

Driving through the park takes a lot of time. And all that time gets me thinking again about the pending eruption of a supervolcano.

A TV show recently featured the top five natural catastrophes that threaten our country. The gigantic New Madrid earthquake fault in Missouri was number three for example.

Number one?

The Yellowstone volcano, of course.

Some scientists compare the possibility of such an event to what is known as "the human bottleneck," which occurred 74,000 years ago when another supervolcano, Toba, exploded on an island off Southeast Asia.

Evolutionary biologists speculate that there were just 15,000 human beings left alive in the entire world after that eruption.

This was one of the solutions given to a DNA mystery: humans are millions of years old, why are there so few different types of DNA?

The conclusion is that 99 percent of all humans were killed in the Toba supervolcano. Every one of us may be descended from those hardy souls who managed to somehow survive somewhere on this decimated planet.

Some controversial DNA scientists, in fact, have identified a male and a female set of chromosomes, which they have designated "Adam and Eve," as our ultimate ancestors.

This theory might give a big boost to those folks pushing creationism over Darwinism.

But since Yellowstone and Toba are two of the most prominent supervolcanoes, well, it got me thinking about such a situation.

I happened to watch one of just about the dreariest movies ever made recently. Called *The Road,* it shows a father and son trying to stay alive in such a decimated world. What they deal with is surely what our world would be like in the wake of a supervolcano.

Oops, back to reality. After staring at the Grand Prismatic Spring, I shook off all those negative thoughts and fears and just soaked up the beauty of Yellowstone.

It was a nice clear day. It was a little windy, but so what? We are in Wyoming, after all.

Or were we? The state of Montana recently captured the image I was watching along with other Yellowstone features and have splashed them in their national tourism ad campaign. Out here in the West, that sounds like poaching to me.

Visiting Yellowstone was like seeing an old friend again. And my friend was in fine form.

This newspaper column was first published in 2011.

Photographer Randy Wagner captures images of erupting Daisy Geyser at left and Clepsydra Geyser in the Lower Geyser Basin, opposite.

Above: In 1997, the Hale-Bopp Comet thrilled northern hemisphere viewers for nearly four months as it traveled west across the night sky. Dewey Vanderhoff captures the comet framed between the stars and iconic Heart Mountain between Cody and Powell.

Opposite: On Christmas eve in 2006, a bighorn ram roamed the sagebrush above the North Fork of the Shoshone River west of Cody in front of the rock formation known as The Holy City in this image also captured by Vanderhoff.

THRONE OF THE MOUNTAIN EAGLE:

Story and photos by Dewey Vanderhoff

On the official USGS topo maps, it is called the "Blackwater Natural Bridge." The writer prefers the "Throne of the Mountain Eagle," for the shape suggested by its aperture and its remote mountaintop "aerie" location. The formation is one of the very largest natural bridges in the world. And it is here in Wyoming.

I have had the good fortune to photograph this amazing wonder many times since the early 1970s. It has been a lifelong source of inspiration. Following is the story of one visit:

The photo below shows Cody horsewoman Deb Hayber during an October day ride to the area. She relaxes on the next ridge over from the volcanic window rock, gazing on what is almost certainly one of the five largest natural arch formations in the world.

Deb is nearly a mile away from the arch in this scene. They are across from one another at 11,000 feet above sea level, located deep in the Washakie Wilderness of the Shoshone National Forest. The Throne of the Mountain Eagle is viewable from many places near and far, but hardly accessible.

What is the size of the Blackwater Natural Bridge? The question remains, since it has never officially been surveyed or measured.

The photos on the bottom right shows the sun in early September, passing behind the Blackwater Natural Bridge from

One of the World's Largest Arches

4.23 miles (22,440 feet) away and 4,000 feet below (according to Google Earth). Given that the angular diameter of the Sun is 0.53 degrees and the arch is skewed away at an angle of about 42-45 degrees in this aspect, some basic trigonometry says the arch spans 285 feet with a thickness of approximately 40 feet. The aperture is about 250 feet tall. These basic calculations do not compensate for refraction, diffraction, or rusty math skills.

Two recently "discovered" arches in China are known to have a definitively greater span. Two sandstone arches in Utah are very similar in size to Blackwater.

The Throne formation is unique among all the world's large arches, due to its high elevation and its composition being volcanic rock, not sandstone or limestone. Technical climbing skills would be required to measure the arch directly. The volcanic rock is also "rotten."

This "bluish" Sun image was taken by photographing the structure through a pair of crossed polarizing filters. As the photographer, please know I was also a land surveyor for ten years and natural history enthusiast. I believe the Blackwater Bridge's span is greater than 300 feet. This is from personal observation on many occasions. Judging size across horizontal distance without control points is difficult.

On the lower right is the same scene during the same sunset, photographed as a "normal" landscape photograph on Kodachrome slide film.

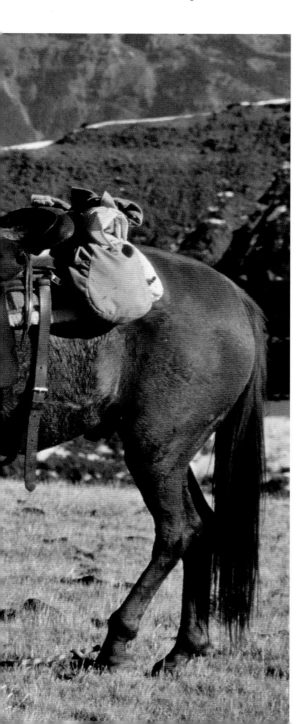

My Grand Teton Park

Beauty and ruggedness define Jackson Hole

By Clay James

Le Trois Tetons.

That's what the early French Trappers and Mountain Men called the Grand Teton Mountain Range in the early 1700s and 1800s.

Since those early visitors, the Valley and mountains have become Jackson Hole and Grand Teton National Park, which is visited by over 3 million people every year. From those early explorers, to the Homestead Act of 1862, to the founding of Grand Teton National Monument in 1929, the valley has experienced many changes and challenges before it became what it is today.

Those early visitors to Jackson Hole were amazed at the beauty and ruggedness of the area. However, it was difficult to survive here, as the weather was brutal and the ground made it impossible to raise crops. Several tried raising cattle but this, too, proved difficult.

But there is some evidence that Native American Indians spent some winters in the "Hole."

The first known homesteaders, John and Millie Carnes and John Holland, were the first settlers to file homestead claims in 1883 and remain through the winter. The first homestead was 160 acres and required that improvements in the amount of $1.25 per acre be made in 5 years. If they did this, they had "proved up" the homestead and were given title to the 160 acres.

The first known white woman in the valley to arrive on her own was Bertha Nelson who arrived in 1888. After that, many adventurous people arrived in Jackson Hole to homestead. Many of the names are familiar today such as Wilson, Nelson, Turpin, Miller, Leak, Simpson, Harrington, DeLoney and the Sheffields in Moran.

Clay James retired from being the CEO of the Grand Teton Lodge Company in 2006 and is a former chairman of the Wyoming Travel Commission. Clay and his wife Shay have spent 37 of the last 50 years in Jackson and now spend part of the year in Arizona.

Opposite: Framed against Mount Moran in the distance, a bison grazes contentedly with four equally contented birds perched aboard. By Daryl Hunter.

Most of the early settlers tried farming or ranching but soon became very discouraged as the soil was very poor and the weather uncooperative. Because of this, many early arrivals moved on and were replaced by newcomers. Many of the newcomers tried irrigation and some of these ditches are still visible today in several valley areas.

As the population of the valley increased, many town sites were started and most had their own schools and post offices. Moose, Moran, and Kelly were early towns that still exist today.

The town of Jackson was organized in 1894 and still is the hub of government for Teton County.

In the early 1900s, the majority of the valley population was still trying their hand at cattle ranching. However, in the early 1920s a large group of ranchers and landowners started a petition to support the creation of a "recreation area" in the valley. A meeting was held at the Maude Noble cabin on the banks of the Snake River near Moose, and the petition was eventually presented to Horace Albright, who was then superintendent of Yellowstone National Park. Mr. Albright had first visited Jackson Hole in 1916 and had wanted to add the Teton Range, which was then part of the Grand Teton National Monument, to Yellowstone National Park.

In 1926, Mr. Albright served as a guide to John D. Rockefeller, Jr. and his wife and sons on a tour of the valley. They had lunch on a hill just north of Jackson Lake Lodge and that hill is now called Lunch Tree Hill.

During the visit, the family became very concerned about the poorly planned and haphazard development that was taking place. Albright presented the Jackson Hole Plan (petition) to Mr. Rockefeller who, soon after, formed the Snake River Land Company to purchase land in the valley with the intention of giving it to the federal government to provide additional lands for a park.

The Land Company was formed to shield the Rockefellers' involvement to prevent specula-

Below: A buck and rail fence frames the Tetons. Photo by Daryl Hunter.

Previous pages: Fall foliage in Grand Teton National Park, by Scott Copeland.

A herd of elk crosses the Snake River, by Scott Copeland.

tion. The Company purchased about 35,000 acres of which 32,500 were eventually included in Grand Teton National Park. It took considerable time for the government to accept the donation and it was not until a proclamation by Franklin D. Roosevelt and an act of Congress in 1950, that Grand Teton National Park was officially established.

Once the park was designated, the Rockefeller family saw the need for visitor facilities and activities. They built the three lodging facilities that still exist: Jackson Lake Lodge, Colter Bay Village, and Jenny Lake Lodge.

These three and several other hotel operations provide lodging and activities for the over three million visitors that come to Grand Teton National Park every year. Activities such as float trips, horseback riding, ranger talks and tours provide the visitors with interpretation and understanding of the park's history and resources.

Several dude ranches still exist that provide a real western experience for their guests. The Rock-

efeller family kept a small dude ranch called the JY Ranch, which they used for family and friends until the early 2000s. This 1,100-acre parcel was restored to its natural condition and donated to the Park in 2007.

Regretfully, today, the family has very little involvement in Jackson Hole but do maintain a small ranch near Teton Village.

Today the Park is about 310,000 acres in size, which is about one-seventh of the size of its neighbor to the north, Yellowstone National Park. It is one of the "Crown Jewels" of the National Parks and is managed by the National Park Service.

It remains nearly the same today as it did many years ago. No new development is allowed and great care is taken by the National Park Service to preserve and protect the park for the use of future generations.

The most impressive part of the Park is the Teton Range, which rises over a mile above the sagebrush prairie. They stand well over 13,000 feet above sea level and have been responsible for drawing appreciative visitors to the park for generations. The Park provides a wild environment that we all need to protect so that we all may enjoy the Park now and in the future.

Opposite: A bull elk bugles under the light of a full moon in this image captured by Daryl Hunter.

Top left, above: A bald eagle feeds its eaglet. Photo by Hunter.

Above: A pouncing fox by Scott Copeland.

Top right: Three bear cubs frolic in the brush, by Hunter.

Right: An elk bugles in Grand Teton Park and appears to shouting into the ear of a nearby bison, by Hunter.

Previous page: In 2003, Tim Doolin captured this elusive image of a moose wading into the Oxbow Bend of the Snake River with Mount Moran in the background.

Above: A moonrise over the Grand Teton, in an image captured by Daryl Hunter.

Below: The majestic Teton Mountain Range can be seen twice in this mirrored image captured by Hunter.

Above: An osprey lifts a very heavy trout as photographer J. L. Woody Wooden snaps this image. The fish was so heavy, the bird needed to make several circles to gain enough altitude to exit the canyon.

Below: A Teton mountain sheep ram beds down against the snow, by J. L. Woody Wooden.

Above: Photographer Daryl Hunter had unique timing when he photographed a grizzly bear eyeballing a bluebird as it wanders through a meadow.

Below: A wolf chases elk in Grand Teton National Park in a vivid image of nature at its wildest. Photo by Daryl Hunter.

Right: Brooks Lake on Togwotee Pass east of Grand Teton National Park is captured by Jared Kail in this image.

Below: Fred Pflughoft has a unique eye for beautiful images of the Wind River Mountains, such as this scene.

Opposite: Square Top Mountain east of Pinedale near Fremont Lake is captured by Paul Ng.

MY SOUTH PASS

Miracle gap in the mountains welcomed emigrants

by Randall Wagner

Randy Wagner, of Cheyenne, was appointed Director of the Wyoming Travel Commission in 1977 and named in 1984 the travel director of the year by the Travel Industry Association of America. He has a life-long interest in Wyoming's historic trails and transportation routes. His 48-year stint as photographer earned him induction into the 2012 Cheyenne Frontier Days Hall of Fame. He and his wife Betty Jean have four children and five grandchildren.

Above: Photo of Randy Wagner by Jan Spencer.

South Pass.

Unique.

North America's South Pass was the key that unlocked the American West to settlement and development. It is the only place on the North American continent where covered wagons, laden with the goods of settlement, commerce and industry, could conquer the Rocky Mountain barrier and the Continental Divide.

Only the South Pass route provided the three essentials for overland travel by draft animal powered vehicles: (1) a constant, daily supply of fresh water for man and beast; (2) a dependable source of grass for the livestock; and (3) a gentle grade to and through the towering mountains, offering no impediment to wagon travel.

Unique.

The discovery of South Pass advanced the nation's "Manifest Destiny" to extend its boundaries "from sea to shining sea" by decades. In the early 1800s the United States ended at the Mississippi and Missouri rivers. From there, west to the Rocky Mountains were the uncharted and unclaimed territories, including parts of Jefferson's Louisiana Purchase. West of the Rockies was Mexico (California, Nevada, Utah, southwest Wyoming, western Colorado, Arizona, New Mexico and Texas). Everything else was "Oregon Country," a huge area that included what is now western Wyoming and Montana, all of Idaho, Washington, Oregon and British Columbia. England held a loose claim to all of Oregon through a scattered series of fur trading outposts that served the Hudson Bay Company headquarters at Fort Vancouver on the Columbia River.

In the early years of the 19th century, there were only two options available to Americans wishing to settle and populate the Pacific side of the continent. The first was a long, tedious, dangerous and expensive ocean voyage around the southern tip of South America, provided a sailing ship could be found and passage could be booked. The second was a 2,000-mile overland journey through unexplored wilderness where no practical path yet existed.

Lewis and Clark had attempted, and failed, to find a rumored "Northwest Passage" to the Pacific. They concluded that a pass south of the route they explored would have to be found if overland travel was ever to be practical. Thus, South Pass was named before it was found.

Unique.

Robert Stuart, a fur trapper in the employ of John Jacob Astor, is credited with the white man's discovery of South Pass. In June of 1812, Stuart and six companions set out on an eastern trek from the destroyed Fort Astoria at the mouth of the Columbia River, bound for St. Louis. On October 12, lost and near starvation, they stumbled through South Pass, eventually finding the Sweetwater and North Platte River routes to the Missouri, arriving home on April 30, 1813. Newspapers reported that the "Astorians" had followed a path that would offer no impediment to overland wagon travel, but Stuart and his companions couldn't remember exactly where they had been. The great South Pass they had found would remain lost for another 11 years.

Unique.

In winter of 1823-24, Thomas Fitzpatrick, Jedediah Smith, James Clyman and a small party of trappers (including a young Jim Bridger)—all in the employ of William H. Ashley—were searching for a way to the west side of the Wind River Mountains. Following Indian advice, they made their way over Beaver Rim and into the mouth of Sweetwater Canyon.

In the days that followed, they rediscovered Stuart's South Pass and made their way into the fur-rich Green River valley, eventually returning to St. Louis by way of the Sweetwater, North Platte and Missouri rivers, firmly establishing the future Oregon Trail route.

Above: Wagons reenact how pioneers crossed South Pass over 160 years ago. Photo by Randy Wagner.

Below: The Oregon Buttes appear in the distance, while wagon ruts are visible in the foreground, by Wagner.

South Pass owes its existence to the Sweetwater River, a product of Wyoming's unique geology. There was a time, umpteen millions of years ago, when Wyoming was a mostly flat, almost featureless landscape. The rivers that appeared were slow flowing, meandering waterways draining in all directions. When the Rocky Mountain building process started, the rivers tended to remain in their established courses, slowly cutting down through the uplifting landscape, eventually forming spectacular canyons that, in some cases, cut directly through newly exposed mountain ranges. The Wind River and Bighorn canyons are classic examples of this action. The Sweetwater, though less obvious, is just as interesting. The Sweetwater River heads on the western slope of the Wind River Mountains and should, by all laws of nature, flow to the Pacific Ocean by way of the Green and Colorado rivers. Instead it diverts to the south, then to the east, forming it own spectacular (though seldom seen) canyon at the foot of the Wind River Mountain range. Farther east, the Sweetwater cuts through another mountain range at a place the pioneers named Devils Gate on its way to the Atlantic Ocean. The Sweetwater River's unusual behavior provided the overland emigrants with the water, grass and gentle grade necessary for their crossing of the Continental Divide, something that could be found in combination at no other place on the North American continent.

Opposite: Devils Gate is a formidable fortress of rock that shrouds the Sweetwater River east of South Pass. Photo by Randy Wagner.

Previous pages:

Spring flowers in bloom at Red Canyon northeast of South Pass. Photo by Scott Copeland.

A lone, wild and vigilant mustang is framed against the backdrop of the Wind River Mountain Range near South Pass, by Copeland.

For the next 16 years, South Pass would serve as the major highway for the Rocky Mountain fur trade. In 1832, Captain Benjamin Bonneville led a rendezvous-bound wagon train through South Pass, the first wheeled vehicles to cross the Continental Divide. On his return, the nation realized that it was now possible to reach Oregon and California by wagon.

The Bidwell-Bartleson Party was the first to try in 1841. Sixty-nine men, women and children signed up for the trip with about half headed for the Columbia River and the rest for California. They made it, but had to leave their wagons on the east side of the Cascade or Sierra Nevada mountains. In 1842 Lansford W. Hastings and Dr. Elijah White led 112 persons on a similar trip with similar results. In that same year John C. Fremont, with Kit Carson as his guide, led the first of four government-sponsored missions to explore and map the west, crossing South Pass on August 7.

The year 1843 saw the Great Migration with over 1,000 Americans on the trail to Oregon Country. Most were in a single wagon train organized by Jesse Applegate with the Willamette Valley as its destination. Most of them made it all the way, wagons intact, to officially open the Oregon Trail through South Pass to emigration and commerce. When thousands more Americans "went westering" in the next few years England quietly gave up any claim it might have had to "Oregon" without a shot being fired.

The storied Donner Party rolled through South Pass in 1846 on their way to a date with infamous cannibal destiny. In 1847 a pioneer party of Mormon Latter Day Saints, under the leadership of Brigham Young, joined the emigration, topping South Pass on their way to a new Zion in the Salt Lake Valley.

In 1848 a sawmill worker discovered gold in California and all hell broke loose. Some 30,000 "Forty-Niners" stormed through South Pass in 1849. By 1852 that number had climbed to 55,000. And, because the overland journey had to be completed between the time that grass turned green along the Missouri River and early winter snow closed the Sierra Nevada passes, all of these gold-fever-afflicted pioneers would cross South Pass within a 3-4 week period, forming an endless wagon train from horizon to horizon. Talk about a traffic jam!

Unique.

By the time the 1869 completion of the transcontinental railroad brought an abrupt end to overland travel by wagon train, more than 500,000 Americans had crossed the Rocky Mountains at South Pass. Most were westbound in search of a new life on the far western frontier. A few were returning east, having failed to find the life they hoped for. In the later years, stagecoaches, freight wagons, Pony Express riders and telegraph, road and bridge builders had become regular users of the South Pass gateway to the West. When it was all over, an estimated 80,000 had traveled to the Willamette Valley in the new State of Oregon, 70,000 Mormon faithful had populated settlements in Utah and the rest, mostly gold seekers, ended up in California and Nevada. America's Manifest Destiny had been well achieved. The United States now extended "from sea to shining sea." Some 55,000 pioneer graves lined the 2,000 miles of the Great South Pass Road in testament to the danger, difficulty and sacrifice of their effort.

Unique.

South Pass continued to provide passage over the Continental Divide for localized wagon trains, livestock drives and commercial freighting operations well into the twentieth century. The wide, well-worn trail of the pioneers gradually evolved into a two-track used by settlers, hunters, fisherman, trappers, rock hounds and

ranchers. It was into the 1950s before the State of Wyoming built the paved Highway 28 over South Pass, connecting Lander and Farson.

The modern South Pass is thought of as a spot on the ground marking the exact place where the Oregon Trail crossed the summit of the Continental Divide at an unimpressive elevation of about 7,400 feet. The pioneers had a different perspective. The historic South Pass was a 30-mile long and 20-mile wide corridor extending from the mouth of Sweetwater Canyon at the base of Rocky Ridge to Pacific Springs on the eastern edge of the Green River basin. It marked the halfway point in their six-month journey, being 1,000 miles west of the Missouri River and 1,000 miles east of the Willamette Valley. South Pass was so wide, long and flat that few knew the exact spot where the Divide was crossed.

Unique.

Crossing South Pass was an emotional experience for many. Pioneer journals are filled with reactions to traveling through the pass, such as, "…today we saw the Sweetwater as a clear, beautiful and swift mountain stream that was beginning to lose itself in the many small branches that make its head. We forded this friendly and accommodating river for the last time and forever took leave of the waters running toward the home of our childhood and youth." Another wrote, "…the thought came to me that, while the good people far away, living in Christian homes and enjoying Christian privileges, were engaged in their afternoon worship, I, in utter disregard of the holy day, was driving an ox team over the roof of the continent." One poetically noted, "…we have reached the dividing line between east and west, the meridian between the rising and setting sun, the mighty landmark midway between our far off homes and the yet distant land toward which our steps are bent." Less impressed, another opined, "…today we have fairly set foot in Oregon Territory …the Land of Promise as yet only promises an increased supply of wormwood and sand."

Today South Pass still exists much as the pioneers left it. Only two small stone monuments mark the actual summit of this most important landmark on the historic emigrant trails. One is dedicated to the Oregon Trail and the other honors two missionary wives, the first white women to cross the Pass in 1836. A Bureau of Land Management fence encloses the summit area and a hand-dug irrigation ditch, intended to divert water from the Sweetwater River to a ranch at Pacific Springs, cuts through the land just north of the summit monuments with a drift fence beyond. A two-track road runs down the center of the impressive wide and deep rut swale that was cut by hundreds of thousands of wagon wheels and then enlarged by wind erosion. A power line is visible to the northwest and some scars from past mining activity are scattered about.

But it's the larger view, the big Oregon Trail scene, described by countless emigrants in their journals, that has changed so little in the South Pass region. The towering, snow-capped Wind River peaks dominate the scene to the north. Looking south, Pacific Butte, Continental Peak and the Oregon Buttes stand as constant reminders of the crossing of the Continental Divide and entry into Oregon Territory. To the east and west, modern travelers can easily find themselves back in the world of the Great Migration, following covered wagon ruts toward an unmarked horizon that never seems to get closer.

You can almost hear the shout, bawl, rumble and whip-crack of the next wagon train. It's a disappointment when one doesn't come rolling over Great South Pass right toward you.

Unique.

Opposite, top: Red-necked phalathropes take flight over Carmody Lake, by Scott Copeland.

Opposite, bottom: Photographer Jeff Vanuga captures the loneliness of a old hag of a tree posing against a backdrop of the north star and other stars. The stars in the night sky rotate around the north star. By setting the camera for a long time exposure, an amazing image such as this can be captured.

Above: One of more ubiquitous inhabitants of the South Pass area is the sage grouse. As energy companies continue to invade its habitat, making sure the bird thrives has become a major environmental concern in Wyoming. Photo by Scott Copeland.

Previous page: Storm over Beaver Rim, by Copeland.

Above: An unusual cloud formation highlights the Oregon Buttes, just south of South Pass. Photo by Mike McClure.

Below: Split Rock is a landmark that could be seen for 50 miles by the early wagon train pioneers along the Oregon Trail. This photo shows it dominating the nearby Sweetwater Rocks formation. Photo by Dan Hayward.

Wyoming is a windy place

by Bill Sniffin

Back in February 2002, my son Michael and I filmed a TV commercial near the Medicine Bow wind farm next to I-80. My recollection is that I was almost blown over by the wind, and we just could not isolate my voice from tremendous amounts of wind noise.

It was during my ill-conceived governor campaign, and although a commercial promoting wind power seemed like a good idea, the ad never ran.

Why? Wyoming had so much coal and natural gas at the time that wind was like a glimmer of hope designed for some time in the future.

My, how things have changed in ten years.

Today, no energy source is hotter than wind, and like coal, natural gas, oil, uranium, and solar—well, Wyoming has an abundance of this energy resource, too.

Of course it prompts the old joke that it is not really Wyoming blowing, but rather just that Nebraska sucks. Ouch.

A recent map showing Wyoming's windiest places reveals a vertical corridor from Converse County south to Albany and Laramie counties as one of the most consistently windy places in the state.

Former Gov. Dave Freudenthal referred to this map as he encouraged the development of wind turbine power. But the key to that development is the ability to connect the generated electricity to the various national electricity grids so we can easily export this resource.

The map shows a vast area in blue (the color for the highest wind speeds) between Cheyenne and Douglas, which is no surprise to people trying to drive I-25 in that area. The windiest area appears to be about 30 miles west from I-25.

Big problem is the map also shows the location for existing power lines, and there are no major power lines in that area, with the possible exception of the Wheatland power plant. The one power line in that area is at capacity.

The governor's advisor on energy back then was former *Casper Star Tribune* publisher Rob Hurless. He says wind is an untapped resource but connecting the turbines to power lines is the biggest challenge in the future.

Thus, where our winds blow the hardest, it apparently is difficult for entrepreneurs to find a place to connect the electricity generated to a power line for shipment to California and other environmentally sensitive places.

Other windy spots include Elk Mountain, Laramie, Rawlins, Wamsutter, South Pass, Wright, east of Evanston, north of Casper, plus a myriad of others.

The state map looks like two halves when seen from the wind perspective.

It is almost like there is a diagonal line running from Big Piney in Sublette County northeast to Buffalo and then straight north of Sheridan. Most everything to the left of this line is not really suited for wind farms (although some Cody people might question that), while the areas to the right of the line show up in bright blues, reds, purples and pinks—all indicating good wind measurements.

One February weekend, I endured some firsthand experience with the wind during a trip from Lander to Casper and on to Cheyenne.

While driving on ice north of Douglas, I went by a pickup pulling a trailer when, oops, in my rearview mirror you could see that he had lost control in the wind and ice.

He drove into the median, throwing up a huge rooster tail of snow. He then drifted into the oncoming lane where he went around twice and jack-knifed. Somehow he did not roll, lose his trailer or hit another vehicle. He restarted his pickup, pulled forward and I last saw him driving down the opposite lane with his right blinker on.

It could be assumed he was going to go pull off the road so he could change his pants.

On our way home, we opted to again take I-25, and were glad we did because I-80 was cleaning up after a 10-car-and-truck pileup that closed the highway. It was caused by ground blizzards from the wind, of course.

This column was first published in 2008.

Below: The wind nearly snatched the camera from Dan Hayward when he captured this super-cell north of Lusk.

Opposite: Reid Wolcott was able catch the sun setting over this unusual rock formation.

My North Platte

A link to our past—and a path to our future

By Mike Enzi, fisherman and U.S. Senator

As every person who has lived in Wyoming knows and every one of the countless visitors to our state has learned, Wyoming is home to a wealth of scenic beauty and natural treasures that just can't be found anywhere else.

The North Platte River is one of those treasures. This is a river that sustained and sustains people, has fantastic topography and diverse wildlife, not to mention fantastic fishing. This is an area steeped in history, but sparsely populated.

That's what comes to mind when I'm driving to meetings in Wyoming and get a chance to stop briefly on the North Platte. For those of us who have to do most of our fishing an hour at a time, usually right beside the highway, the North Platte offers lots of opportunities. It wanders in at the middle of the southern border of Wyoming at an elevation of 8,845 feet as a rushing small stream. It's joined by many tributaries and becomes a river by the time it reaches the first of the dams. Then the river makes a sweeping turn to the east in the center of the state and exits the state halfway down the east border at an elevation of 4,080 feet on its way to the Missouri and then the Mississippi and then the Gulf of Mexico.

Wyoming enjoys some 350 miles of fishing, water recreation, backpacking, camping and habitat essentials for moose, elk, bear, deer, antelope and smaller animals like beaver, coyotes, rabbits, raccoons and others. There are a lot of birds to be seen here, too: geese, ducks, sage grouse, pheasants, golden and bald eagles, and a variety of hawks. All are "Worth the Watching" (a Wyoming slogan). There is an official count of the huge variety of birds done on the same week of every year.

The North Platte is one of the best fisheries in the world, with some 3,000 trout a mile surveyed throughout much of the river: brown trout, rainbow trout, brook trout, and of course, the native cutthroat trout. It's a fisherman's dream. That's why the North Platte river system is high on any fisherman's list of favorite places. No one knows how the cutthroat got here, but it's not hard to understand why they decided to stay. The river provides every kind of water from white water to deep pools, to languid prairie water to lakes. As you fish you will smell sagebrush and pine and see scattered pockets of quaking aspens that turn to golden shimmers in the fall.

It's always best to fish with a friend or—if you're lucky—your grandchild so you can experience fishing for the first time all over again through a young child's eyes. Also, in case there are any disputes, you have a witness who can attest to the truth of Grampa's latest fish story. A grandchild is a lot better than a camera and lot easier to convince. If I tell him it was a seven pounder, I'm sure he'll back me up in future stories. I do use an Abel Measure Net, invented in Wyoming, so the length is never in dispute. Doing "catch and release," my grandson is convinced I know some of the fish by name and have a sense of their family's roots. He seems to be totally fascinated by his Grampa's knowledge of the creatures who call the river their home.

The first people who encountered the North Platte must have been just amazed by the sight of these waters. As you approach the river, the sound of the rushing water captures your attention and you feel an immediate sense of reverence for this magical place, a sense of awe and respect that amplifies your anticipation. The sun plays on the water and shimmers like diamonds as it dances on the surface.

There are traces of people in the area near the Platte River system as far back as 11,000 years ago. There are actual campsites here that date back to as long ago as 2,500 years. The North Platte provided all who came here with a wealth of opportunities and resources they would need to care for themselves and any animals.

The North Platte was already inhabited by American Indians when the first explor-

Mike Enzi grew up fishing the waters of Wyoming with his grandfather and father. Currently Wyoming's 20th U.S. Senator, he started his own business (NZ Shoes) in Gillette with wife Diana after he completed an accounting and marketing degrees. Mike and Diana have two daughters, one son and four grandchildren.

Right: An aerial view of the North Platte River north of Saratoga by Dan Hayward. The white cliffs of Sheep Mountain are in the top portion of the photo.

ers came through Wyoming. Then explorers became trappers. Then traders came to save trappers the long pilgrimage to St. Louis and the East, to trade beaver and then buffalo hides for supplies. The Western migration brought people through the area making historic trails, the river being the main map. The Pony Express followed part of the North Platte, shortly replaced by the telegraph. The Transcontinental Railroad sent "tie hacks" up the North Platte to cut logs for railroad ties and float them down to the rail head to build track in the race across Wyoming. Then gold and copper brought miners. The railroad brought farmers and settlers. Towns began to form as central places for supplies.

Before Fremont and Sublette and other traders came West, the trappers interrupted their year to use this river "road" to St. Louis for their fur-laden canoes. When I've canoed the river on a time schedule for a pick up downstream, it's frustrating to only see a river bank instead of landmarks to tell how far you've come. Trappers didn't even have maps to know where they were. I wondered how they could stand it until I realized they didn't have a time deadline. They got in the canoe in the morning and paddled as long as they could. At night they would pull the canoe up on a shore, climb up the bank and say, "This morning I was on that side of that mountain. Tonight I'm on this side of it. It was a good day!"

I need to introduce you to the towns on the North Platte formed because of the river. Following the closest road to the river, it's 45 downhill miles with rapids from the Wyoming border to Saratoga (population 1,726), which still has an old fashioned ice cream parlor in the Wolf Hotel where rooms can still be rented without a bathroom.

Be sure to say hi to Hack at the fly shop by the bridge and take time to soak in the hot springs by the river. Another 20 miles brings you to Walcott (population zero), which has only a filling station. Then it's 17 miles to Sinclair (population 433), the home of the Sinclair Refinery. Next, drive 31 miles of local paved road and 36 miles of gravel road and 12 miles of local paved road to Alcova (population 20) with a fly-fishing shop, a restaurant, a rural school, some homes, the

The rugged carved walls of Fremont Canyon south of Casper are captured in this photo by Stephen Schlager.

gateway to Alcova Reservoir, marina, the Grey Reef and Miracle Mile of fishing, as well as fantastic float trips.

Next, go 35 miles to Casper (population 55,316), the second biggest city in the state, and home of Casper College, the National Historic Trails Interpretive Center and the museum at Fort Caspar for a feel for the early days. Casper was once the site of a ferry [a big raft on a rope], about the only way for miles to get wagons and animals to the other side of the river. Follow the North Platte on Interstate I-25 for 17 miles to Glenrock (population 2,231) whose slogan is, "Big enough to enjoy—Small enough to care." Go 21 miles to Douglas (population 5,288), an original habitat of the jackalope (a cross between a jackrabbit and an antelope), home of the Wyoming State Fair, and the final resting place of Sir Barton, the first thoroughbred colt to win the American Triple Crown.

Next is 29 miles to Glendo (population 229) with the slogan, "Small in number—Big in heart!" sitting on the edge of Glendo Reservoir with a marina. Drive 34 miles (you leave the interstate after 19 miles) to Guernsey (population 1,147) where you can still see the ruts from wagon train days.

They have a golf course you can play for $22 a day ($12 more for a cart) or play 14 consecutive days for a total of $132, including the cart. It's 13 miles to Fort Laramie (population 243), originally established as a private fur trading fort in 1834, crossroads of a nation moving West. It became the largest and best-known military post on the Northern Plains, abandoned in 1890, but preserved and restored. Then 20 miles to Torrington (population 6,501), the home of Eastern Wyoming College and 8 miles from where the river flows out of the state. Wyoming only has 14 towns where the population exceeds the elevation, and three of them—Casper, Douglas and Torrington—are on this river.

Farming and water encouraged irrigation of this high desert area. Dams producing electricity were built to store water and reduce flooding and to turn mud-churned water to crystal clear, fish-supporting, sustained flow. Irrigation canals take the water to where it is needed.

It's not hard to imagine the pioneers, having left all civilization behind, feeling relieved that

Opposite: Glendo is one of the five major reservoirs on the North Platte River as it works its way through Wyoming. In the distance looms the massive Laramie Peak. Photo by Randy Wagner.

Previous pages:

A snowy scene such as this one can occur often in summer months in the Medicine Bow Peak area. Jonathan Green snapped this photo in July 2011.

This panoramic photo frames an unnamed red butte, which stands above the valley floor west of Midwest and north of Casper. Photo by Tim Doolin.

the river assured they were headed in the right direction, a much needed feature for the pioneers, travelers and explorers who were headed West. The waters probably provided their food and water while providing the basics of life that today we find at the local store. Back then, the North Platte was the local store. I can imagine they would stop to refresh their horses as it offered them an opportunity to hunt the wildlife that was in abundance here.

Even today it's not hard to imagine what life was like for those heading West as they passed near these waters and headed along the Oregon, California and Mormon Trails. The Pony Express route went nearby, too. A lot of the North Platte's scenic beauty is pretty much just like it was when the early pioneers were trekking through.

You won't find a lot of condo projects bragging about their view of the river. We believe in leaving some things alone—and we have done that for huge stretches of the river, thanks to working ranches that protect open spaces on much of the river system. People come to visit Wyoming every year to get a sense of what this country was like back in our early days.

The waters move along at a real good clip. It's a reminder of the great power that can be harnessed here. In Wyoming alone, the North Platte provides an enormous amount of hydroelectricity. The energy the dams provide equates to the amount of electricity needed for 72,000 homes. That power comes from 15 major dams and reservoirs. It also provides some much-needed water to about 3.5 million people along the way. The states surrounding the river have come to depend on its water. The dams cleaned up the river and hold water until needed for irrigation of a land considered a high desert— irrigation water to more than 440,000 acres of land in Wyoming and Nebraska.

When Mark Twain said, "In the West, whiskey's for drinking, waters for fighting over!" he probably had the North Platte in mind. Through the years, there have been disputes between Wyoming and Colorado and between Wyoming and Nebraska, beginning in 1911 with the latest, but not last, decision issued in 2001.

Even though we're now so far removed from those early days when Wyoming wasn't yet a state, when you're fishing here it's very easy to lose yourself for a moment in the thought of all those settlers headed West in search of a new life. It had been a very difficult journey even to this point. It was dangerous and there was always a potential threat just ahead. For them, just about everything was unknown. The animals were wild and dangerous. The trappers and other people who liked the isolation could be unfriendly. It was more than an adventure. It was an expression of faith that somehow you'd be guided along safely and eventually find your way to Oregon or California or Utah.

There's a lot to be said for the bravery and the courage of all those who faced those perils and still continued their journey West. There's also a lot to be said for the wisdom and good old-

Right: A natural bridge over La Prele Creek is subject of a photo by Randy Wagner.

fashioned common sense of those who discovered Wyoming, fell in love with all it had to offer and decided to stay here. If they came through in May, after the spring rains, they would find lush green valleys. The high desert dries everything out in August—but it was too late to move on then. The next year the cycle would repeat. Only the really hardy ones stayed.

The North Platte is truly one of Wyoming's greatest treasures. It provides electric power and water for recreation and agriculture. It is a place for families to enjoy that perfect afternoon outdoors. It's also a vital link from our past to our future as a state and a nation. It reassures us that no matter how tough things may be, we can boast of our ancestors who made it through worse.

Visitors seem to sense we're made of the same stuff that made our pioneers brave to the point of being fearless. Living here breeds the kind of gentle but firm confidence and strong faith that we learn from this land of wonder. Many generations will be sustained mentally and physically by this river.

The timeless waters of the North Platte serve as a constant reminder of those days of long ago as it reassures us to face our future with hope. There's no better place to be than on or near the North Platte.

And if you are really quiet, perhaps you will hear the whispers of those who have gone before us; a reminder that God had everything carefully planned for this place so it would create an instant replay memory that would keep us coming back for more.

That is the lure of this "Wonder of Wyoming," the North Platte River.

Above: Scott Copeland caught this image of four mule deer bucks in the North Platte River Valley.

Below: The famous Miracle Mile fishing area of the North Platte River is photographed by Randy Wagner.

Above: A lonely, windswept tree serves as a sentinel overlooking Seminoe Reservoir, one of the main reservoirs on the North Platte River. Photo by Randy Wagner.

Above: Ominous storm clouds loom over Muddy Gap in this photo by Reid Wolcott.

Opposite: Snowy Range scene by Rick Carpenter.

MY DEVILS TOWER

"Close Encounters" with a geological wonder

By Gene Bryan

Pick a topic: American history…Wyoming history…Military history…Geology…Native American lore…Wildlife…Mountain climbing…Motion Pictures…Tourism…"First in Outdoor America."

A geological phenomenon tucked away in the Black Hills of northeast Wyoming can make a strong case for notoriety in any one of those topics. Devils Tower National Monument has a secure place in American history as the nation's first national monument, but this Wyoming icon (think Old Faithful, the Tetons, Wyoming's bucking horse) has earned a niche as a Wyoming natural wonder and treasure.

Gene Bryan's four-decade tourism career began in 1967, and included stints with the Wyoming Travel Commission, Cheyenne Frontier Days, and the Cody Chamber. He was inducted into the Cheyenne Frontier Days Hall of Fame in 2006. He and wife Jeannie live in Tucson.

Randy Wagner quickly snapped this photo of Devils Tower as fog lifted for about 20 seconds over the country's first National Monument. This image was used for years as a poster for the Wyoming Travel Commission.

Rising like a giant tree stump out of the Black Hills of Wyoming, the Devils Tower and its nearby cousins, the Missouri Buttes, dominate a region of rolling forested mountains, the Belle Fourche River and belly-deep grassland that provide habitat for an array of wildlife (mule and whitetail deer, wild turkeys) and commercial beef cattle and bison.

Not to go James Michener on you with too many details, but the Devils Tower dates to more than 200 million years ago. The oldest rocks date to the Triassic Period, and the startlingly beautiful red rock formation (the Spearfish) is made up of sandstone, siltstone and shale. About 65 million years ago, during the Paleogene Period, the Rocky Mountains and Black Hills were uplifted. Molten magma oozed through the earth's crust and solidified. Erosion over the last many millions of years exposed an igneous intrusion or laccolith we know as the Devils Tower. It rises 1,267 feet above the Belle Fourche River and surrounding ranchland, and its summit stretches to 5,112 feet. As erosion continues, more and more of the Tower will be exposed.

The Tower and Black Hills regions of Wyoming and South Dakota have played integral roles in Native American history and spirituality,

especially for the Kiowa, Lakota Sioux, Cheyenne, Crow, Shoshone and Arapaho. There are literally tens of different Indian stories of how the Tower was formed. The Kiowa and Lakota Sioux believe that several young girls went out to play and were chased by giant bears. The girls climbed on a rock and prayed to the Great Spirit to save them. The Great Spirit caused the rock to shoot into the air, and the bears, in their attempt to get the girls, carved the columns on the tower walls with their giant claws. Still another version involves young boys, and again the Great Spirit saved them. A painting depicting this story by artist Herbert Collins hangs above the fireplace in the visitor center at the Tower.

Not surprisingly, the Native Americans have a whole host of names for the geological wonder. Bear's Lodge, Bear's House, Bear's Lair, Grizzly Bear Lodge, Bear's Tipi, and Mateo Tipi are among the more colorful.

It is assumed that some of the early fur trappers probably visited the area, but the first documented visitors were several members of the Captain W.F. Raynolds' 1859 Yellowstone Expedition. About 16 years later an expedition led by Col. Richard I. Dodge came to the Tower to study the geology, and during the visit the expedition's interpreter misinterpreted the Native American's name to "Bad God's Lodge," which was later shortened to "Devils Tower." After Dodge's expedition brought attention to Devils Tower, Congress moved to set the area aside as a U.S. forest preserve in 1896. Then, on September 24, 1906, President Theodore Roosevelt, the "conservation President," signed legislation designating Devils Tower as the nation's first national monument. This act solidified Wyoming's position as "First in Outdoor America" as the Tower joined the world's first national park (Yellowstone) and the country's first national forest (Shoshone).

Interestingly, in today's "politically correct" environment, there have been attempts to change the name. The most recent came in 2005 when it was proposed that the monument be re-named

The Bear Lodge National Historic Landmark. Then Wyoming Congresswoman Barbara Cubin led the successful opposition.

The Native Americans' close connection to Devils Tower and the Black Hills has led to conflict over the years with a popular form of outdoor recreation: mountain climbing. A pair of area ranchers—William Rogers and Willard Ripley—are credited with the first documented ascent of the Tower. On July 4, 1893, the intrepid duo used a ladder of wooden pegs wedged into the cracks on the rock faces to find their way to the top. Remnants of their wooden ladder are still visible today from the hiking trail that encircles the monolith. In 1941, a publicity seeker, George Hopkins, parachuted (without permission) onto the Tower. Bad weather moved in quickly, and he was stranded for six days before a climbing party plucked him off the Tower. One can only imagine the choice words the National Park Service had for Mr. Hopkins!

The Native Americans, particularly the Lakota Sioux, Kiowa and Cheyenne, consider the Tower sacred ground and have objected to the hundreds of climbers who flock to the Tower. After considerable discussion and negotiation in the late 1990s, a compromise was reached that leaves the Tower climber-free during the month of June when the tribes conduct their religious ceremonies.

Like most Wyomingites, I imagine, during my early years with the Wyoming Travel Commission I had a stronger affinity toward Wyoming's two "crown jewel" national park properties—Yellowstone and Grand Teton—than with Devils Tower. That changed when I made my first extended trip to Devils Tower in the early 1970s with the Commission's assistant director/photographer Jim Simon. Jim was a brilliant, very private individual who had carved out a storied career with the Wyoming Game and Fish Department, Rockefeller Game Preserve and Walt Disney Productions. He was not one to spout his considerable knowledge without being asked. I had the good fortune, as News and Information Director, to accompany him on a four-day field trip to Crook County. We criss-crossed virtually every inch of that history-rich, geology-endowed, wildlife-teeming county from Devils Tower, Missouri Buttes,

Sundance, Hulett, Belle Fourche River, Sand Creek and Ranch A, the mining ghost town of Welcome, Vore Buffalo Jump, Aladdin with its mercantile and nearby mining tipple, Beulah, and all points in-between. It was an indelible and invaluable education for a green-as-a-gourd tourism marketing "student."

No account of the Devils Tower would be complete without mention of one of the area's pioneer ranching families. It was also during the early '70s that I first met ("encountered?") the Driskill family of Crook County. Ranching homesteaders literally at the foot of Devils Tower, the Driskills' history in the area is nearly as rich as that of the Tower. The family has raised hay, beef cattle and more recently American bison for more than three quarters of a century. I initially met Jesse and his wife Ellen when they owned and operated one of the country's first KOA Kampgrounds, located smack at the entrance to the monument. And, speaking of icons, Jess is the epitome of the American cowboy—hard-riding, tough talking, work like a fool from sun up to sun down, dog and saddle his best friends and drink a little whiskey. The Driskills became loyal supporters and occasional critics of the state's travel promotion program, but, more importantly, good friends. Ellen died in the late 1990s and is buried in the shadow of Devils Tower in the Driskill Family cemetery on the ranch.

Ironically, when Governor Dave Freudenthal re-instated the Wyoming Tourism Board in 2002, he selected me and Matt Driskill, Jess and Ellen's youngest son, as original members of the new board. My connection to the Driskills had been re-kindled. My wife Jeanne and I have spent three Fourth of July holidays at Matt and Kathy Driskills' KOA Kampground. We have spent countless memorable hours with Jess, Matt, Kathy and their daughter Jessie and brother Ogden and his family during those stays. The Driskills stage one of the finest free barbecue dinners and spectacular fireworks displays (bar none) on the 4th. One of the highlights is catching the flicker of lights coming from climbers who have attached themselves to the wall of the Tower as they watch the fireworks from their lofty perches.

A "must" during any stay at the Devils Tower KOA is the opportunity each night to re-visit

Following pages:

An HDR image of Devils Tower becomes a work of art. This image was created by Ken Stoecklin. HDR is a photography technique that utilizes different ranges of exposure.

Lightning is not uncommon in the Devils Tower area or at any mountain range in Wyoming. Here a series of lightning bolts is captured during a time exposure by photographer R. L. Woody Wooden.

Fall colors dominate this panoramic scene in the Bighorn Mountains in Johnson County with the Bighorn and Darton Peaks soaring above, by photographer Tim Doolin.

Above: Devils Tower and an old cabin in the area. Photo by Randy Wagner.

Below: The tower is silhouetted against a red sky in this image by Dan Hayward.

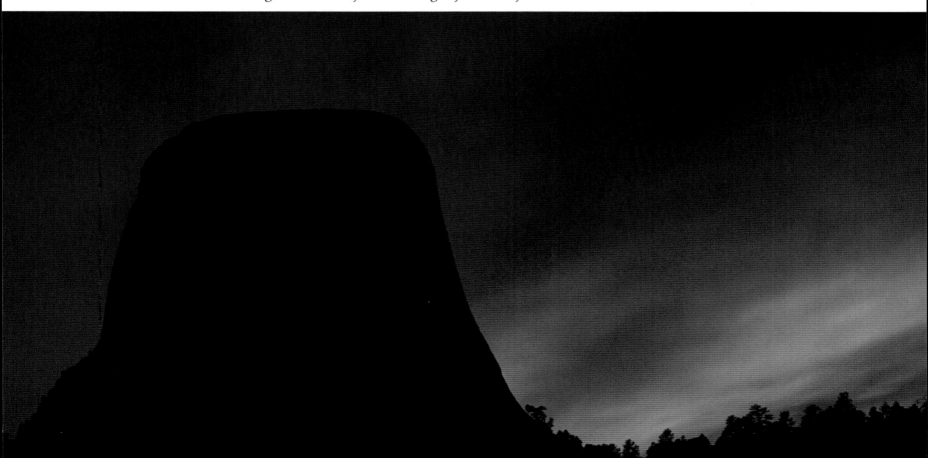

Several bull moose browse through willows below Twin Buttes in the Big Horn Mountains near Burgess Junction. Photo by Tim Doolin.

Opposite: Crazy Woman Canyon is one of the favorite places to visit outside of Buffalo in the Big Horn Mountains. Photo by Ken Stoecklin.

the 1977 motion picture "Close Encounters of the Third Kind" on the deck outside the restaurant. No telling how many copies of this Stephen Spielberg classic, starring a young Richard Dreyfuss, the Driskills have consumed. Nonetheless the Devils Tower is the non-speaking "star" of this science fiction thriller. It is no exaggeration to say that "Encounters" has had an enormous impact on the visibility of and visitation to Devils Tower since '77. Even today, when "Encounters" is telecast, anywhere in the world, inquiries to the state tourism office spike upward.

Tragically, Matt Driskill was killed in a freak accident at the campground one month after we left him after our last Independence Day ad-

venture in 2011. His ashes were scattered near his beloved Devils Tower.

The 1,346-acre national monument can be reached off Interstate 90 via U.S. 14 from either Moorcroft to the west or Sundance to the east or by taking a marvelous loop drive by exiting Interstate 90 at the Aladdin Exit 12 miles east of Sundance and taking Wyo 111 and 24 thru Aladdin, Alva and Hulett to the Tower. Make certain to visit the sparkling new Wyoming Welcome Center, located on the westbound lane of I-90 at the Aladdin Exit, to learn more about the wonder that is Devils Tower National Monument and the rich heritage of Crook County, Wyoming.

My Wyoming bucket list

By Bill Sniffin

We live, we die, and the wheels on the bus go round and round. —Jack Nicholson

Figuring out what you want to do before you die was the theme of a popular 2008 movie called *The Bucket List,* starring Jack Nicholson and Morgan Freeman.

I found the movie inspiring and immediately put together my own "Wyoming Bucket List"—those places in our great state that I would like to experience before kicking the proverbial bucket.

Now, my portfolio of places in the state already visited is terrific. Readers of this column have shared vicariously some of those experiences.

We experienced some doozies in 2007. For example, it was my first time visiting the Medicine Wheel. And that trip involved the mind-boggling scenery of US Highway 14A from Lovell to Burgess Junction.

This past summer was my first time to travel that exotic road between Saratoga and Laramie. It also marked my first visit to the original Hobo Spring in Saratoga.

As a long-time aficionado of Flaming Gorge, this past year was my first-ever visit to the Firehole area, a Grand Canyon-like location at the north end of the 91-mile long lake.

Perhaps in the early 1970s I once drove on Highway 191 south of Rock Springs, but I have forgotten it. In 2007, we took that journey and wow, the vistas were expansive, to say the least.

There were probably a few other "firsts," last year, but what I want to share with you now is my list of things that are on my Wyoming Bucket List for the future. Here goes:

• Hoping to get back to Frontier Days—there is nothing like this event in the world.

• The Vedauwoo area outside of Laramie deserves a closer look. Again, I have driven by hundreds of times. Also, to spend some time at Curt Gowdy State Park.

• There is a man-made rock arrow in the Red Desert that points toward other ancient teepee rings. It is between Jeffrey City and Wamsutter and will make a nice quadrunner trip.

• Between Jeffrey City and Muddy Gap is an odd rock formation I call Stonehenge. Reportedly it has names written in it, including John Sublette. Sometime soon it will finally get checked off.

• Our family lived on Squaw Creek outside of Lander for 23 years, and our view looked out at Red Butte. Hope to climb it.

• If Fossil Butte is not on this list, my friend Vince Tomassi will let me have it. He serves incredible meals every Thursday night in Kemmerer-Diamondville at Luigi's. Perhaps a tour and dinner, Vince?

• I have snowmobiled Yellowstone a couple of times but not for 20 years. Hope to do that again.

• The Killpecker sand dunes north of Rock Springs are unique. Sounds like another great quadrunner trip.

• In 1993, I spent a very nervous time hunting a bighorn ram in the Double Cabin Area northeast of Dubois.

Would love to go back for a more relaxed trip this time around.

• Some 40 years ago, I photographed what looked like a horrible scar on Togwotee Pass when the area was clear-cut. Would like to go to those areas and see if the timber has recovered.

• Is there anyone out there who might give me a tour of the "breaks" north of Lusk? I flew over that area by private plane many times and looked down in awe at this rough country.

• Northeast Wyoming is an interesting area, especially Keyhole Reservoir and the Vore Buffalo Jump. Would like to spend some quality time around Devils Tower, too.

• A tour of Wyoming's giant coal mines makes sense.

• Would like to do some fishing in Bighorn Canyon.

• It is easy for me to get LaGrange and LaBarge confused—perhaps I need to visit them.

• On the Wind River Reservation, I would like to visit the Arapaho Ranch and also visit the mountains at the extreme north end of the rez.

• And finally, I want to spend some quality time in Bill, Wyoming.

So that's my Wyoming Bucket List. What's yours?

READERS REACT TO COLUMN

Wow, a snowmobile trip on the Continental Divide Snowmobile Trail and a trek along the old stage trail from Saratoga all the way to Montana were two of many offerings presented when I asked readers of my weekly newspaper column for "their" Wyoming Bucket Lists.

With all this input, some very good ideas have been added to my bucket list.

Former Landerite Wendy Jacob wants to snowmobile the amazing Continental Divide Trail, although now that trip requires a permit to cross Yellowstone in winter. That trail, which consistently is rated one of the best in the USA, runs from Lander's Sinks Canyon over to Pinedale and back across the Wind River Mountains to Togwotee Pass and then across Grand Teton and Yellowstone, finishing in West Yellowstone. There are some areas now that need some ferrying, but the trail is still one of the greatest in North America.

I always wanted to do that ride, too, but alas, perhaps in another life.

Lowell Ray Anderson wants to follow that stagecoach road that goes through places I have never heard of, Embar and Blonde Pass. Sounds like an ambitious trip.

Former Wyoming Tourism Director Gene Bryan added "camping out in the most beautiful place in the state"—at Green River Lakes below Square Top Mountain in the Pinedale area. He also wants to re-visit the Red Desert with local historian John Mioczynski and also hike to Hidden Falls behind Jenny Lake at the foot of Mount Moran. "Those will serve as starters," he concludes.

The late Bill Wilson had a goal of visiting every state park and historic site. Laura Nelson Martin also has the goal of visiting all the old forts in Wyoming. Now those are great Bucket List goals!

Former Fremont County Attorney Ed Newell plans to

bike the Wyoming section of the Continental Divide Trail. It will be his chance to see "Wyoming's backcountry, border-to-border," he says.

Jared and Joanna Kail took their young daughters on a GPS-guided trip to locate the exact center of Wyoming. Sounds like a great trip.

Butch Egger wants to go back to the Hole in the Wall. He went there 15 years ago "when George Taylor owned the Willow Creek Ranch." He says his great-grandfather Mike Bader was a cook and a lookout for the Wild Bunch back in those pioneer times.

Lois Herbst, long-time rancher near Shoshoni, has a fear of heights but would love to have someone take her up on the Chief Joseph Highway and also to the sky-high Medicine Wheel. I think there are some folks out there who just might help her out.

Kathy Browning wants to take her family to Devils Tower, which she has never seen. They are in for a treat. That whole area offers so much. She also wants to do Yellowstone in winter with her kids. John Lichty is taking a friend from North Carolina on a snowmobile trip to Old Faithful as part of his bucket list.

Mindi Crabb wants to ride the length of the Wind River Mountains "with my sweetie," spending many weeks catching lots of trout. Watch out for the mosquitoes!

Phil Noble wants to play every golf course in the state. Fore!

So there are some more great ideas.

What do you want to do for your Wyoming Bucket List?

Originally published in 2008.

Above: A younger and bearded Bill Sniffin fulfilled an earlier bucket list goal by visiting a petrified forest above the Double Cabin area east of Dubois in 1993. This was at 11,000 feet. Photo by Dan Kinneman.

Right: 33-Mile Road in the Hole-in-the-Wall country west of Midwest. Photo by Tim Doolin.

Below: Wild sumac flames brilliant red beneath the Needles Eye in Tongue River Canyon in the Bighorn Mountains near Dayton. Photo by Doolin.

Opposite: At 11,926 feet, Spar Mountain, near Kirwin, towers over Cascade Canyon and Smuggler's Gulch and boasts a host of colored soils revealing the presence of multiple minerals. Heavily saturated from a recent rainstorm, the bright colors and textures create the appearance of brush strokes, making the image resemble a painting more than a photo, by Doolin.

MY RED DESERT

The loneliest place in the loneliest state

By Jim Smail

A former Jeep dealer and state snowmobile trails director, Jim Smail of Lander now works for the U.S. Forest Service. Smail is a wonderful storyteller and knows all the famous and infamous history of Lander Valley, the Red Desert and the Shoshone National Forest. He visits the Red Desert as often as possible.

Opposite: Wyoming has several major wild horse herds. Here, two stallions, who brought their mares to a watering hole at the same time, fight to determine who gets first access to the water on a hot August day. Photo by J. L. Woody Wooden.

My Scottish grandfather came to America and homesteaded back in 1915. He started taking my father to the desert back then and that tradition continued on to me when I arrived on the scene 75 years ago.

Has this magnificent area known as the Great Red Desert changed in the three-quarters of a century that I seemingly have been roaming it?

Well, yes and no.

Just like today's energy prospectors, the desert was always seen as a place of opportunity. In typical risk-reward activities, the stakes were high when you ventured out into this vast empty place.

As a place almost devoid of permanent human habitation, it has been the scene of Oregon Trail travelers, gold prospectors, the Pony Express, the first telegraph poles, and other intrepid souls trying to conquer an unconquerable place.

Geographically, some folks think the desert is a gigantic space that includes land crossed by Interstate 80 and extending up toward Casper, Shoshoni, Riverton, and Lander and encompassing Rock Springs and Green River.

But to the purist, and I guess that includes me, the real Red Desert is the confines of the Great Divide Basin. This, truly, is the loneliest place in the loneliest state. A place with no permanent human habitation at the present time. Despite that, it is a place that had been occupied by humans for thousands of years.

In many ways the desert has not changed at all.

Among the high points of my life has been driving my jeep around the desert and visiting ancient sites of these early humans. We always approach these places with respect and with a vivid imagination to try to figure out what was happening here.

Perhaps this desert affection started with some

family history. My dad climbed up Boars Tusk north of Rock Springs and sat me in the notch high above the desert floor when I was just 18 months old. Now that would whet anyone's appetite!

To someone speeding by the desert on the highways, well, how can you describe to them the joys of White Horse Canyon? Or the vast Killpecker Sand Dunes? The magic of Steamboat Mountain and its wondrous buffalo jump? Adobe Town or the Honeycomb Buttes? Continental Peak and the famous Oregon Buttes? And so much more.

It is a vast area and once you start looking, well, it is almost impossible to comprehend it all.

Here's a challenge: turn on your Google Earth app on your computer, tablet or smart phone, and scan the Red Desert between Rock Springs and Lander. What you see will look like the surface of some far-away planet. Yet, it is right here.

Let me take you on a little journey that we took earlier this summer. Here are some of our thoughts and feelings.

Strange noises and odd winds abound in the desert. Was that sound just the wind or was it the noise generated by the ghosts of a vast herd of bison that roamed this place for thousands of years? Or was that the cry of a lonely Indian brave in the center of a vision circle evoking whatever image he was trying to conjure?

Maybe it was the plaintive cry of the gold miner lost in a snowstorm, knowing full well that his death was imminent. Maybe it was the sound of a lonely mountain man trying desperately to work his way across this vast expanse alive.

Perhaps it was a combination of all of these.

We were standing on a lonely knob about 25 miles southwest of Jeffrey City.

Strange rocks covered this knob and, occasionally, powerful gusts of wind would come from nowhere and almost knock you down. My three companions and I all looked at each other following these gusts. "What the heck was that?

Did you feel that?" I was driving the author of this book, Bill Sniffin, around to some of these odd sites. It was his first time out here to most of them. He was experiencing the odd feelings and powers that the desert emits.

But we were not there to check out the wind. Unusual ancient rock structures and symbols were our goals.

Instead of the more common term "teepee rings," I prefer the term "vision circles," which can be found in old sites along old, worn Indian trails.

My theory is that young Indian braves or perhaps older Indian medicine men used these circles as ways to experience visions or to communicate with the spirit world.

Instead of perfectly round circles, often the rings of rocks would have an opening and most often, they actually had a spiral effect, as if "to let the spirits into the circle."

Although I do not qualify as a learned college professor, I have spent much of my 75 years in this desert, having originally grown up in Farson and spending the rest of my life in the Lander area.

We continued on riding along the well-worn trail to a rarely visited location near the Honeycomb Buttes. There, we found 19 of these vision circles, which were the best I had ever seen.

We were in the northern part of the Great Divide Basin, a vast 2.25-million-acre area where the Continental Divide splits in two. Water inside that basin does not go outside of it, not East or West.

Wyoming is the lowest populated state in the country. And the least populated place in Wyoming is this basin.

Sniffin's favorite area in the Red Desert is the Oregon Buttes area, which is full of wondrous rock formations and strange canyons. He contends that if Wyoming had a vortex area, it might very well be right there.

Aging hippie-types like to believe that certain places in the world have special energy fields called vortexes. Not sure I believe it, but there are places that sure give me a positive energy boost.

Opposite: Mexican Hat Valley in Adobe Town is captured by Paul Ng.

Then another of our companions, Joe Motherway, told us about these weird circles he and

his wife Bonnie had found. We headed off to the east through this maze of old dirt roads and two-tracks. Occasionally there were roads blocked by signs listing that area as part of a wilderness study area. We are not allowed to drive off the road with a jeep or ATV.

This new spot was hard to find and after a miss or two, we finally arrived. And then the afore-mentioned wind really started to blow. Eerily so.

The place was littered with what Joe called "Flying Saucer Rocks," which appeared to have been burned and had other little rocks stuck to them. The site was a small barren knob sur-rounded by dozens of square miles of sage-brush.

It was obviously a special place. And it was full of these vision circles—only these really fea-tured that spiral effect. Doubt anyone would call them teepee rings because of the odd shape.

Of course, we did not disturb them. Just took some pictures and tried to keep from getting blown over by the wind.

Then it was time to go home. We traveled a few miles before stopping. "Do you notice anything different now?" Joe said. "No wind."

Right: Old roots reveal the harshness of life in the Red Desert. Photo by Ken Driese.

Below: The reason the Green River is called by that name. This image was taken by Bill Sniffin just south of the town of the same name.

Opposite, top: Killpecker Sand Dunes, by Reid Wolcott.

Opposite, bottom: The view from the summit of one of the Oregon Buttes reveals an interesting topography by Eric Molvar.

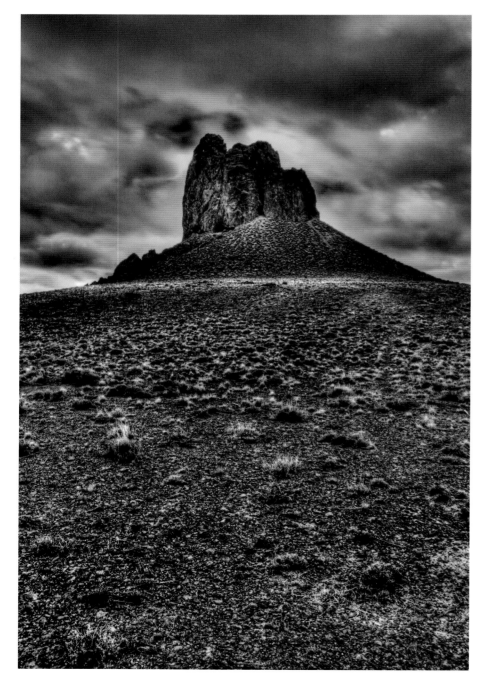

Rock Springs-based photographer R. J. Pieper took the photos on this page with left showing the Killpecker Sand Dunes, lower left is the famous Boars Tusk rock formation and above, "looking through the looking stone" at the south edge of the Red Desert.

Previous pages:

A panoramic view of a sunrise at the Honeycomb Buttes by Scott Copeland.

Bill Sniffin snapped this panoramic image of the Firehole Canyon area of the Green River just north of Flaming Gorge.

Above: Hells Half Acre is one of the more unusual places in the state and was even the site of the movie Starship Troopers a few years ago. Photo by Randy Wagner.

Opposite: Ken Stoecklin created this colorful image of the desert during its green spring phase.

Above: Antelope with twin fawns populate the Red Desert. Photo by Scott Copeland.

Below: Ken Driese photographed the sand dunes near Ferris Mountain. The dunes stretch across the central part of Wyoming.

Above: A hoodoo rock formation just north of Baggs photographed by Bill Sniffin.

Below: Fossil Butte is a national monument near Kemmerer. Photo by Randy Wagner.

Above: Castle Gardens is an spectacular rock formation east of Riverton that also contains some of the most amazing petroglyphs in Wyoming. Photo by Randy Wagner.

Opposite, top: Dan Hayward photographed these beige-colored, petrified sand dunes near an area called Chimney Rock.

Opposite, bottom: About the only positive result of forest fires is the resulting amazing sunsets. Here, Michelle Motherway captures the Bears Ears rock formation near Dickinson Park west of the Wind River Indian Reservation in Fremont County.

MY THERMOPOLIS

Why it's easy to love the world's largest hot spring

By Pat Schmidt

Because of the surprises! Geological, paleontological, archaeological, recreational, educational, developmental, meteorological, physical, even emotional!

For decades travelers through Wind River Canyon have learned about its formations that reveal millions of years of geologic time, thanks to roadside signs.

Motorists entering Wyoming's last frontier, the Big Horn Basin, emerge into its colorful southern tip and more geology lessons.

Pat Schmidt is a past editor and publisher of the Thermopolis-Hot Springs Independent Record and The Lovell Chronicle. His civic involvement includes serving on the Wyoming Business Council Board of Directors. A Greybull native and a graduate of the University of Wyoming, he is a decorated veteran of the Vietnam War. He and his wife Emily have three children and seven grandchildren.

Opposite: The "Big Spring" at Thermopolis in all its colorful glory by Jonathan Green.

Shades of red accent the mini-mountains surrounding Thermopolis Hot Springs. (Imagine the relief that travelers over the centuries must have felt when they realized the smoke they spotted at the northwest edge of the valley was actually steam rising from a concentrated area of hot springs known by the Shoshone People as Bah-gue-wana, Smoking Waters.)

Those fascinated with the beauty of the area often overlook the geological story told by the many ages of terraces around Hot Springs State Park. After walking the Rainbow Terraces, follow the Spirit Trail or drive just to the north; a closer look near the White Sulphur Spring will reveal extinct former hot springs pools and giant terraces, even a mini-geyser cone.

Look west across the blue-green, trout- and turtle-laden Bighorn River at T Hill and Roundtop Mountain. You'll see less obvious travertine terraces formed thousands of centuries ago.

Two retired geologists in Thermopolis, Barbara and John Vietti, suspect the next travertine terraces are starting to form below the Rainbow Terraces. To see evidence, visit the Hot Springs in the coldest part of winter. Because of the warm waters flowing from Boysen Dam, the river seldom freezes over in the Canyon or Thermopolis. When it does, a portion of the center of the river below the Swinging Bridge never freezes. Could it be hot mineral water rising in the river, starting a new travertine terrace?

Plastic liners under the shallow Rainbow Terrace ponds have been used for several decades to try to stop water from leaking through rather than running over the terraces.

Measuring the water flow over the decades has been difficult. Minerals coat the inside of measuring devices, and the water leaves the Big Spring in a ditch and three subsurface pipelines. The state engineer measures the water and, to protect the spring, also limits the drilling of new wells within roughly ten miles of the Big Spring. Flows are now in a period of decline.

The $60,000 agreement withdrawing an area of approximately ten square miles from the Wind River Indian Reservation that became Thermopolis Hot Springs was negotiated in 1896 between delegations led by a U.S. Army Major, Inspector James McLaughlin, Shoshone Tribal Chief Washakie and Arapaho Tribal Chief Sharp Nose. However, the proposed pact was left dangling while the U.S. Congress debated what to do its acquisition.

The agreement required the "Big Horn Hot Springs" be set aside "as a national park or reservation" for the use and benefit of the public and the Indians. Over a year later the Federal government and Wyoming finally worked out an arrangement for the state to administer an area of approximately one square-mile around the Big Spring as a "Reserve."

Pioneers squatting near the springs or living in Old Thermopolis and Andersonville several miles north outside the earlier reservation boundary were finally able to start building what is now Thermopolis on the other nine square miles of land purchased from the tribes.

Most visitors to Hot Springs State Park don't realize the county fairgrounds, grade school, high school, athletic fields, skate park, armory recreation building, county library and senior

citizens center are within the western boundary of the state park.

Close to a million people visit the main part of Hot Springs State Park annually, mostly in the warm months. Among Wyoming's state parks, studies prove it generates by far the most economic benefits for Wyoming.

The winter months arguably are the best to visit and warm your bones. The hot mineral water, mild winds, and lower elevation of Thermopolis lead some to call it the "banana belt" of Wyoming. There are few sights to rival the park's trees and structures coated with hoar frost or ice, created by snowfall or steam rising from the Big Spring. And youngsters of all ages treasure catching snowflakes in their mouths while swimming in warm mineral water.

It's hard to imagine what Thermopolis Hot Springs would be like had the Federal government decided to keep the area as a national park. That protected status might have preserved some of the hot springs such as the one that some say was lost when the railroad cut its way through on the west side of the Bighorn River.

On the other hand, Hot Springs State Park is an outstanding example of cooperation between private enterprise and government. Would travelers stop for more than a few minutes if there were only some terraces and a hot spring?

Instead, private investment has built two swimming complexes with their water slides, varied swimming pools and other attractions. State management and investments in the spectacular grounds, bathhouse, pavilion and other facilities add to the attractions.

Much of the park is within the Town of Thermopolis, resulting in further investment by the community and its citizens. An example is the Riverside Walkway that was built by local volunteers, organizations and businesses.

The promise in the 1896 agreement for free use of the hot mineral water is fulfilled in the state bathhouse nestled below the south edge of the Rainbow Terraces. Anyone may soak in its indoor or outdoor pools, and there are two private areas equipped for people with special needs.

The public may also enjoy the hot mineral water from the Big Spring at four commercial locations: the Star Plunge; Hellie's Teepee Pools; the Days Inn Convention Center, with its stun-

ning display of world wildlife; and the Best Western Plaza Inn.

Other facilities just inside the south boundary of the park are the Wyoming Pioneer Home, the Gottsche Wellness and Fitness Center, and Hot Springs County Memorial Hospital.

Creation of the other outlets for the mineral water, the two Teepee Fountains, probably wouldn't have been allowed in a national park. They date back to 1909 when steam stopped the flow of hot mineral water through water lines. Tall pipes were installed as steam relief valves, using a small block structure. Over the decades, minerals from the water deposited the same travertine as in the terraces, creating the spectacular, colorful giant cones of today.

While the health benefits of drinking the mineral water were touted in the early 1900s, just one drinking fountain remains, alongside Buffalo Street east of the Wyoming Pioneer Home.

Until a decade ago, outdoor ponds were used to cool the hot mineral water to temperatures used in the pools. Because of fears of contamination by animals and humans, an enclosed heat exchange system was built.

Cool water is taken from the Bighorn River and piped to a building above the bathhouse. There the cold river water flows through coils to cool the hot mineral water. After being cooled, the mineral water flows to the pools and bathhouse. The river water, slightly warmer after the process, goes into the former cooling ponds and flows back to the river.

Current park superintendent Kevin Skates is quick to point out the bathhouse and pools use "only 100% pure mineral water from the Big Spring because it is so naturally perfect for health reasons."

In earlier days, people who felt their health had been restored by bathing in the healing waters would hike to the top of the hill above the Big Spring and place rocks on cairns there, leading to the name Monument Hill. Hikers still may register at the one cairn on its top. The "World's Largest Mineral Hot Spring" sign on its side was created with rocks in the 1930s.

In 1916 the Swinging Bridge was built to link the Rainbow Terraces to the highway side of the park and a now long-gone hospital. Regrettably the railroad was allowed to remove a smaller

Opposite, top: The overall scene of the Thermopolis Hot Springs by Lara Love.

Opposite, bottom: The Teepee Fountain, which is a steam relief valve created by Mother Nature and coated by travertine for over 100 years.

footbridge over its tracks that completed the popular hiking route.

Both T Hill and Roundtop are public areas with special protection. In the summer months, a small segment of the state buffalo herd is moved to the T Hill Natural Area to avoid interbreeding. Roundtop Mountain includes a park named in honor of the donor, Lewis Freudenthal, father of former Wyoming Gov. Dave Freudenthal. To wander the trails of the King Spiller Butte Relic Site below the southwest corner of T Hill, pick up a pass at the county extension office.

Among the many walking and hiking routes is a Volksmarch course that starts at the state bathhouse.

At one time, visitors could also view elk and bear inside the park; only the state buffalo herd remains. It was started in 1916 with 15 cows from Kansas and a bull buffalo from Yellowstone National Park.

Extinct creatures are the latest Thermopolis Hot Springs surprise. Just 18 years ago, dinosaur experts on their way to view fossils elsewhere stopped to examine the Morrison formation on the ridges southeast of Thermopolis. They found the treasure trove that led to creation of the world class Wyoming Dinosaur Center and Dig Sites. The museum displays come from those hills and from around the world, including the collection of co-discoverer and founder Burkhard Pohl. There is also a sister museum in China.

The exhibit that is most rare, known internationally as "the Thermopolis Specimen," is one of only 11 Archaeopteryx. The fossilized creature links birds and dinosaurs and is found in fossil beds in Germany. This is the only Archaeopteryx in the Western Hemisphere.

Adults, students and children travel to Thermopolis from around the world to study the specimens, tour the museum and dig sites and even dig for and discover new dinosaurs.

Scattered petroglyphs can be found in the hills around Thermopolis, but the famed Legend Rock Petroglyph Site, just over 30 miles west, has close to 300. It is managed as part of Hot Springs State Park.

The Gift of the Waters Pageant the first weekend of August at the Big Spring is a reenactment of the Shoshone Nation blessing the hot

mineral water before the transfer of the lands to the federal government.

Additional recreational opportunities include trophy trout fishing in the Wind/Bighorn River, whitewater trips through Wind River Canyon on the Wind River Indian Reservation or a gentle float through Thermopolis. The Hot

Right: Dan Hayward captures a rainbow over Camelback Rock.

Following pages:

This panoramic photo by Tim Doolin is a reminder of the cycles of life. This upturned elk antler and skull bears testimony to the unforgiving harshness of nature on a windswept ridge above Yellow Creek near the headwaters of the Greybull River in the Washakie Wilderness near Meeteetse.

One of more mysterious places in Wyoming is the "Sinks," where the Popo Agie River disappears into the mountainside and reappears downstream a quarter of a mile later. This panoramic image by Scott Copeland was snapped southwest of Lander.

Springs County Museum is one of the best small-town facilities anywhere.

Douglas has its jackalope; Thermopolis Hot Springs has the Wedding of the Waters for its humor. Two streams don't merge at the mouth of the canyon. Wedding of the Waters "explains" the mistake made by explorers and map makers in the 1800s who didn't realize the Wind River could find a way to cut north through a couple of mountain ranges and be the Bighorn River in Montana.

Most of all, I love that special feeling, the warmth of being home in a part of Wyoming I love when I emerge from Wind River Canyon and reenter the Big Horn Basin, no matter how long I have been gone.

May it be the same for you!

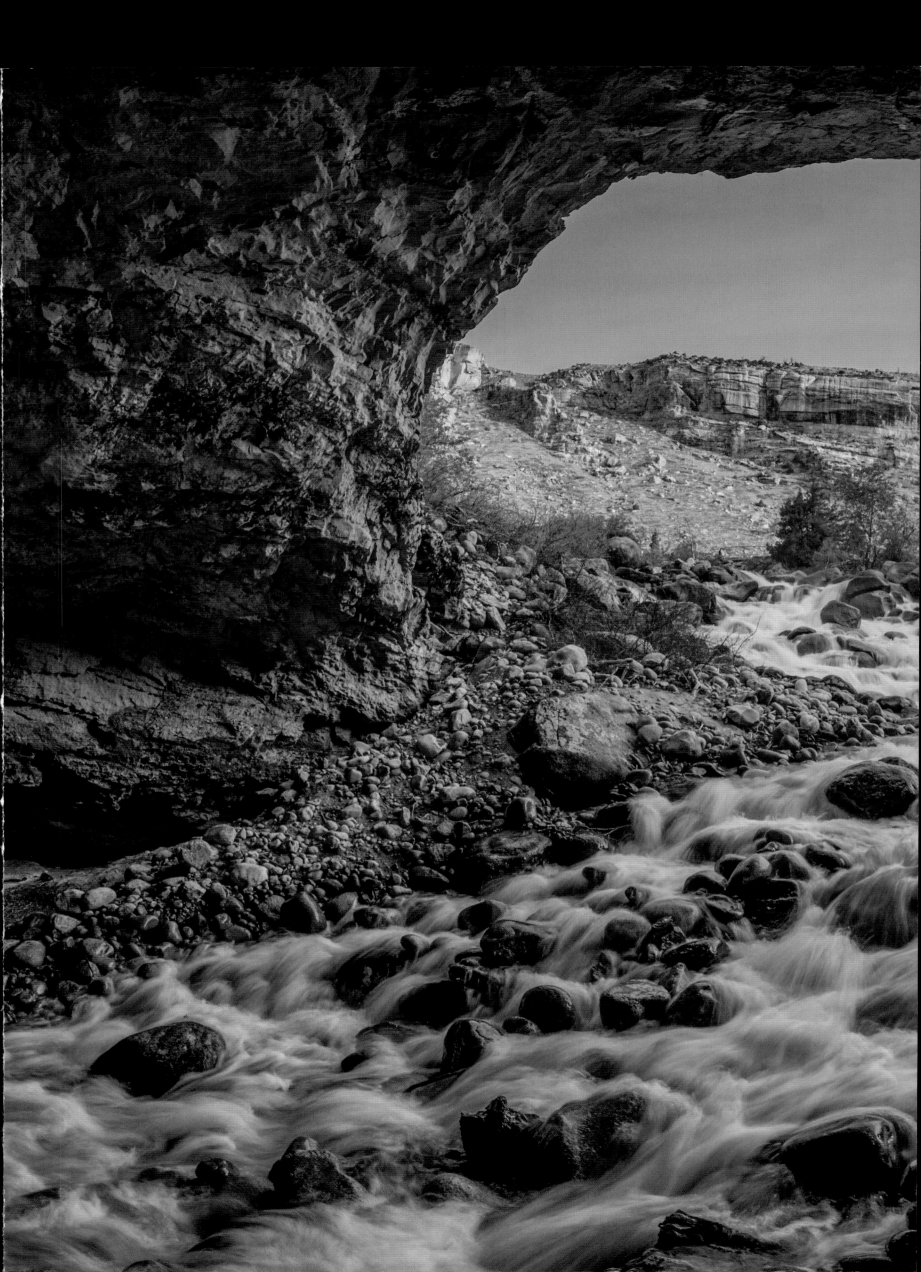

A Wyoming love story

by Bill Sniffin

"Go West, Young Man." —Famous admonition by New York Publisher Horace Greeley in the 19th century

Below: Bill Sniffin captures rainbow in full glory over Lander.

Opposite: Below: Old Chief Mountain is framed by a gibbous moon in this image by Dewey Vanderhoff.

I'll never forget the first time I saw Wyoming in the daylight. It was in September, and we were in Lander after arriving late the night before, having flown from Iowa to Denver to Riverton.

We looked out the window of the Holiday Lodge and saw the bubbling Popo Agie River below us. In the distance the Wind River Mountains soared. The air was clear, and the sun was shining brightly. We could hardly wait to get going.

As we drove around town in our rental car, we marveled at the clean streets. And they had no patches in them. It was almost like this town had brand new streets. They were the widest streets we had ever seen.

Yes, they were new. Lander had only had paved streets for two years!

No wonder they looked so good.

The town, with its unlimited water usage, featured the greenest yards ever. Back in Iowa, a lot of yards had burned up due to limitations on sprinkling.

Wyoming was unique to us. And Lander looked even more unique. This most unusual of small towns was a jewel, with its manicured green lawns, its spectacular wide streets and its mountain valley setting. This looked like a place a person would want to move to someday. The sooner the better.

Neither Nancy nor I had ever been to the West before. We had never seen mountains or experienced the blue skies and low humidity that make this part of the world unique.

We visited Sinks Canyon, and the beauty was just overwhelming. The Popo Agie sparkled as it bounced over the rocks. I was seeing with my eyes the same images I had seen on magazine covers, never realizing that this is how it really DOES look in real life.

We kept looking at each other and thinking, "We could really live here."

Our time in Iowa had been fruitful, but it was time to move on. It was 1970, and we were itching to grow. Mr. Greeley's famous admonition was a true guiding light for me. I was 24, Nancy was 23 and we had been living in Harlan, Iowa, her hometown.

Two things gnawed at me: a desire to move west and a desire to own my own newspaper. A man named Bruce Kennedy needed a publisher for the Lander newspaper and offered to fly Nancy and me out here to look it over.

So we visited Lander and liked it a lot. I would be the fifth publisher in two years, and the job was a terrific challenge. The staff was virtually leaderless, and although they worked hard, they really didn't know the business very well.

One thing will always stick in my mind about how they produced the Lander paper. When the staff was done putting together section B, they would start on section A. And if they didn't have enough news, they would just go back to Section B and pull out a few stories and re-run them again in Section A. I had never seen that done anywhere before, and once we arrived, the *Lander Wyoming State Journal* never did it again.

After our three-day visit to Lander, we drove to Greybull, where Kennedy lived. We told him we would probably take the Lander job.

He was also involved in the Gillette newspaper and wanted us to visit that town. After that visit, we looked at the map to see how far it was to Casper and, although I had a half-tank of gas, I figured I could gas up at Pine Tree Junction.

Wrong.

The only thing at Pine Tree Junction was a pine tree.

We had to beg some gas from a construction worker in the camp called Bill so that we could finish our trip to Casper. We missed our flight and spent the night there before heading back to Iowa to give our friends, family and co-workers the news that we were heading west.

It's been 42 years since all that happened. And those first images Nancy and I had of our adopted state of Wyoming and our adopted hometown of Lander are just as vivid today as they were then.

We love it here and will always make it our home.

We weren't born here. But we got here as soon as we could.

This newspaper column was first published in 2007.

Wyoming is where the wild things are

By Bill Sniffin

The Loop Road in the Shoshone National Forest above Lander is one of the lesser-known and yet most spectacular tourist places in the state.

But in my four decades here, it never seemed possible that the Loop would be a place to encounter both grizzly bears and wolves. But, alas, it is now true.

The Wyoming Game and Fish Department has confirmed a photo taken by a bear hunter's motion-

Above: A sow grizzly with a rare set of triplet cubs was photographed by Daryl Hunter.

activated remote camera. It shows a five-year-old grizzly roaming around a timbered area on Fairfield Hill. This is the hill on the right side of Sinks Canyon, seven miles from Lander at the start of the Loop Road.

Farther up Sinks Canyon (named for the mysterious "sinks," where the Popo Agie River disappears underground and reappears a quarter of a mile down the canyon) are the "switchbacks," a series of back-and-forth turns up Fossil Mountain. This is the beginning of the Loop Road. The road takes travelers on a 25-mile journey through the Shoshone National Forest, emerging at

Highway 28 on South Pass.

On the second switchback, local dentist Dr. Eric Sheridan saw two wolves frolicking recently. This is just one of many recent sightings of wolves in the southern Wind River Mountains.

Never in my wildest dreams did I think we could have grizzlies and wolves in our backyard. Heck, my neighbor in the city limits of Lander even swears he found a wolf track in his garden.

Friends and relatives who are seemingly more enlightened tell me to embrace this wonderful influx of wildlife.

So, gulp, I guess that may be my new attitude.

But I wanted to write about what a fantastic and unique resource our wild animals are in this state. Let me share a few experiences:

• I am a former chairman of the Wyoming Travel Commission. We in the tourism business embraced the Game and Fish campaign called "Wildlife Worth the Watching."

Our commission always pushed extensive tourist surveying along with our former long-time director Gene Bryan. We discovered tourists loved coming to Wyoming to see our wildlife almost as much as the big parks, high mountains and vast deserts.

I once suggested to our tourism marketing folks to use the term "America's Serengeti" to describe our vast herds of antelope, deer, elk and bison. They never used it, but I sure did to describe our unparalleled wildlife vistas to potential tourists.

What a visitor sees when coming to Wyoming is unique in the Lower 48. I have traveled extensively in Colorado, Utah and Montana, where you do not see such herds of animals.

• Another unique sight is our herds of wild horses. Although not

natural residents, they still offer a breathtaking look at what life is like in the wild.

The Sweetwater County Tourism Board has done of marvelous job of promoting tourists seeing the Red Desert herd, as have folks in the Lovell area.

• Now let me tell you about a typical Wyoming day I had recently at my home, which is a small acreage on the edge of Lander but *within* the city limits.

As I left my house at 7:30 a.m. to meet with my coffee group, known affectionately as the Fox News All-Stars, I watched a mule deer doe give birth to a fawn. The little guy wobbled and stumbled but pretty soon was nursing and hoppity-hopping away.

Pretty special, huh?

Later, on my way back to my house on the same driveway, a hen pheasant and her brood of tiny chicks held me up, bopping along down the lane in front of me.

Later that morning, I had to stop for a youthful fox that was frolicking around.

Earlier this spring, we had a professional trapper remove two beavers that had mowed down a dozen trees and blocked the creek. They weighed 60 and 40 pounds and were transplanted to the national forest, where there were plenty of other beavers.

We have lived in our present location for 12 years but saw our first bald eagle in May, slowly flying over our backyard. We hear this bird is a permanent resident of the Popo Agie River area.

What happens at our place may seem unique, but in reality it happens all across Wyoming. We Wyomingites do live in a wildlife paradise.

So I guess, in my old age, it might not make sense to complain about the arrival of grizzly bears and wolves. I still am not happy about it but am trying to rationalize that if we like living where the wild things are, and, we do, well...

This newspaper column was first published in 2011.

Above: This eagle was captured by J. L. Woody Wooden with a 1,000 mm lens while still 160 yards in the distance.

Below: Photographer Jeff Vanuga captured the speed of a wolf running in this unusual image.

Tips for living in Wyoming

By Bill Sniffin

By all indications, population growth has been steady here in Wyoming and will be increasing.

So what tips can we come up with to help out these new folks headed our way?

It was just 42 years ago when our family moved here, and let me use that experience as a partial example:

• What the heck is a barrow pit? Well, here in Wyoming, that is the area along the roads where dirt was gathered up to create a roadbed. But back in my Iowa hometown, we call that a ditch. Here, a ditch is a groove in the land that carries irrigation water.

• The "pass is closed because of bad weather." Really? Hard to imagine the possibility of a pass being closed here in the 21st century? If you are coming to Wyoming, you better darned well believe it is closed.

• What are mineral severance taxes? Newcomers have heard of property taxes, sales taxes and income taxes, but what is this? Newcomers should learn about it, since taxes on our minerals amount to about two-thirds of all taxes paid here.

Those are just three things that seem to be pretty much unique to Wyoming.

The Wyoming Humanities Council not long ago decided they could help out newcomers and visitors, too. That august group felt some kind of primer was necessary for newcomers to our state. What should be in such a guide?

Probably one thing would be the admonition to keep your mouth shut when you attend your first public meetings.

Our old-timers are insufferably polite, but it is almost impossible to not think: If it was so great where you came from—why did you leave there and come here?

So what other unique Wyoming tips would you offer someone who is moving here? I asked some folks and here is what they said:

Scott Goetz of Lander says we need to explain to people what those odd fences are. Jo Anne McFarland of Riverton says that when she first told newcomers they were "snow fences," they thought she was kidding.

Clay James of Jackson says to buy a good strong snow shovel. Diane Galloway, who moved from Wyoming to Washington, D. C., says she always packed a survival kit in her car for winter trips.

Rancher Jim Allen reminds that good fences make good neighbors. Wyoming is a "fence out" state. It is your responsibility to fence your property so other people's livestock do not trespass on your land.

Former Iowan Tom Lacock of Cheyenne says that you should keep your gas tank at least half full, especially in winter. "Just because there is a dot on the map does not mean there's a gas station there."

Dave Kellogg of Lander says you need to make sure the spouse is prepared the kind of erratic weather you can get here. University of Wyoming Professor Phil Roberts echoes that you better learn to appreciate the Wyoming wind. Bob Peck of Cheyenne says get used to "horizontal snow." And if you do not know what directions are, just look at the trees, "they all point east."

Chris Boswell of Cheyenne said when he first moved to Wyoming (to Green River) it was somewhat intimidating to see all the bumper stickers that read Wyoming Native. But the town was welcoming, and all those people stayed and have families full of new Wyoming natives.

State Treasurer Joe Meyer recalls taking new state officials around the state and advising them "to just listen." He also suggested they read *Rising From The Plains* by John McPhee.

Scott Ratliff of Riverton says it is great to have a state where you can have a good career without needing an advanced education, thanks to the mineral industry.

My sister Susan Kinneman, formerly of Dubois, says newcomers do not understand all our acronyms, like BLM, USFS, G&F, EPA and DEQ.

And finally Debbie Hammons of Worland offered: Do you know the story about the guy in Wyoming who had a small convenience store? A newcomer stopped and asked what the folks were like in the town. The owner asked, "What were folks like back where you're from?"

"They're really small-minded, closed to newcomers, gossip a lot."

"Well," said the owner. "That's about what you'll find here."

That fellow left, and another newcomer pulled in. He too asked what folks were like here. The owner replied with his same question, "What were folks like where you're from?"

"Oh, they're great," said the fellow. "Open and hospitable, help you out if you need it but respect your privacy."

"Well," said the owner, "that about describes the folks here, too."

First published June 1, 2008

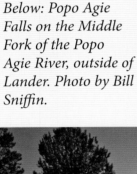

Below: Popo Agie Falls on the Middle Fork of the Popo Agie River, outside of Lander. Photo by Bill Sniffin.

Above: Curtis Zablockic descending the "Owen Spaulding" route on the Grand Teton, by Bobby Model.

Below: Tent with star trails under the Merlon (a satellite of Cloud Peak) in the Bighorn Mountains, by Model.

Above: A lonely leaf glistens in this image captured by Mike Smith of some fast running water.

Below: R. J. Pieper captured Flaming Gorge with the stars from the Big Dipper looming overhead.

Above: Grey's River has a blue sheen to it in this image by Paul Ng, taken in the Star Valley area.

Below: Rock formations off Blue Bank Road near Worland, by Dan Hayward.

Wyoming's "High Altitudes, Low Multitudes"

By Bill Sniffin

Below: Shell Falls, by Fred Pflughoft.

Previous page:

One of the most exciting wild horse roundup photos ever taken. This image was captured by Dewey Vanderhoff near the Pryor Mountains by Lovell.

Once, when I was speaking to a group a long way from home, someone asked me if I was "lonely."

"No," I replied. "I am alone. But I am not lonely."

That could also sum up how Wyoming people feel sometimes. We live in this vast state with fewer neighbors than anywhere else in the continental United States.

The 2010 census once again proclaimed Wyoming as the least-populated state in the union. Some 565,000 hardy souls claim to live here. If they all lived in one city, it would still be smaller than some nondescript places named Huntsville, Fresno and Gary.

There have been documented cases of busloads of foreign tourists pulling over to the side of the road to stare out at our vast acres of "nothing." We've even heard about cases where these tourists can get reverse claustrophobia—they get physically sick by the absence of walls, boundaries, noise and thousands of other human beings.

Those of us who call Wyoming home chuckle to ourselves when we hear about such things. We aren't alone. And we aren't lonely, either. My favorite slogan for Wyoming is:

High Altitudes.

Low Multitudes.

Let's talk about those high altitudes. There are mountains higher than Wyoming's, but are there places more beautiful than the Tetons? Or the Cirque of the Towers? Or Square Top Mountain?

Our state is full of wonderful mountain ranges like the Big Horns, the Wyoming Range, the Snowy Range, Casper Mountain and even the Pryor Mountains.

I love all our funny buttes, like Dishpan, Pilot, Crowheart, Black, Pumpkin and Fossil.

Perhaps the most famous of these kinds of odd bumps are those stubby Oregon Buttes located on South Pass between Fremont and Sweetwater Counties.

Some 350,000 people literally jumped off the edge of the earth when they headed west on the Oregon Trail from 1848 to 1866. They headed out with the good intentions of our nation's manifest destiny. They were going to a new land.

The first real mountain they saw was Laramie Peak in eastern Wyoming. But the ones they really wanted to see were the Oregon Buttes. These bumps on the horizon marked South Pass. They knew if they could get over South Pass before winter hit, they would be pretty much home free—no storms could freeze them now. These squared-off buttes were probably the most famous mountains in America during that two-decade time period. And those buttes sit right in the middle of Wyoming.

I have been covering news in Wyoming for over 42 years, and I have heard the phrase "High Altitudes, Low Multitudes" from probably a half-dozen prominent political figures during this time.

Former Gov. Jim Geringer always added: "…and great attitudes," when he recited it.

Here in Wyoming, it isn't hard to have great attitudes. When you live in a place where the sky is blue 300 days per year and the sun shines brightly, well, that makes for our sunny dispositions. And the humidity is so low that old cars in our state are greatly valued around the country because of their lack of rust.

We could consider these two lines as a possible new state slogan, even. It could offer a reverse psychology approach to marketing Wyoming after all, when tourists want to go on vacation, they usually want to escape the hustle and bustle of their busy lives.

For years, Wyoming put a huge billboard on one of the busiest traffic stretches in New York City. It showed a picture of downtown Lander with a herd of cows holding up traffic. The caption read: Traffic jam in Wyoming.

The theory was that anyone trapped there in that modern traffic jam might want to yearn to be out here in Wyoming, away from those crowds.

What people all over the country don't understand about Wyoming people is that we actually like it this way. We actually choose to be in a land where the antelope outnumber the humans.

On the subject of slogans, during our occasional severe winters, you might think that our state slogan goes like this:

Strong winds

Blowing snow

Slick in spots

To wrap this up, I like to quote another of former Gov. Mike Sullivan's favorite descriptions of Wyoming: "It's just a small city with extremely long streets."

This newspaper column was first published in 2009.

Above The White Horse rides out from the Red Castle at dawn. The volcanic butte, located 20 miles southwest of Cody is Castle Rock, also called Colter Rock. You can see a distant snowbank in the shape of a white horse, the fabled "Ishawooa Horse's Head" snowbank whose distinctive melting form determines when high water crests on the Shoshone River. When the horse's reins appear to "break," high water has passed. By Dewey Vanderhoff.

Below. A mountain lion snoozes on a ledge north of Yellowstone. Photo by Scott Copeland.

Above: Three climbers reach the summit of Wyoming's highest mountain Gannett Peak. The patch of snow they are climbing on is the same patch that can be seen on the top of the summit of the photo at right of Gannett, in all its glory.
Photos by Scott Copeland.

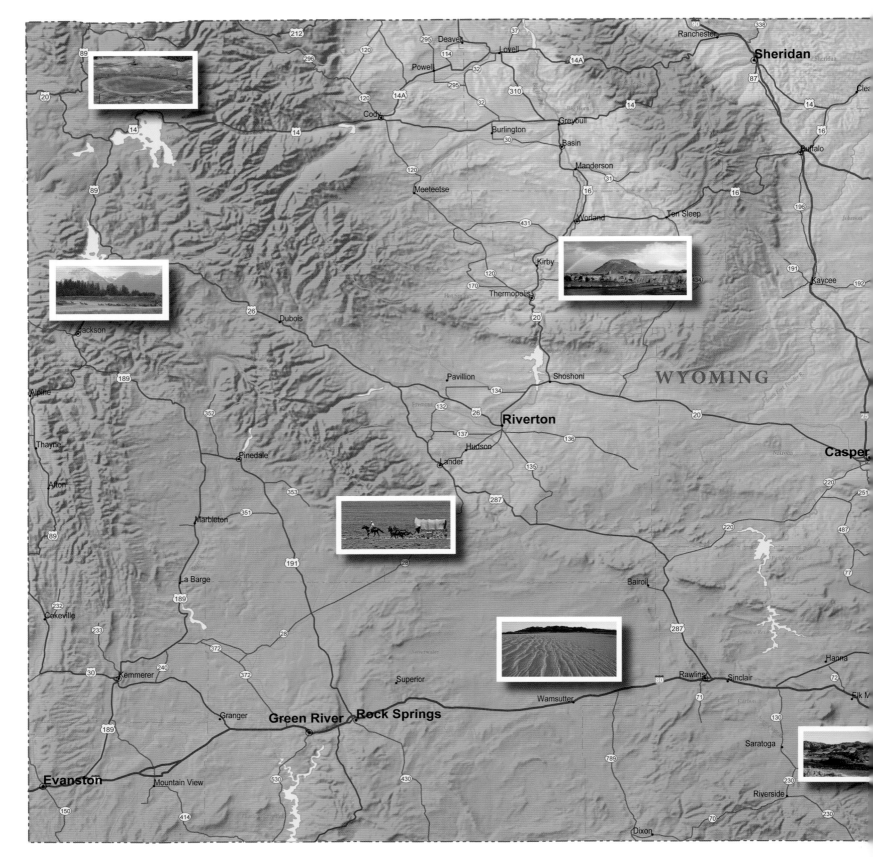

WYOMING

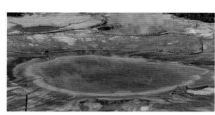

My
Yellowstone Park:
pages 8-33

My
Teton Park:
pages 34-53

My
South Pass:
pages 54-71

My
North Platte River:
pages 72-89

My
Devils Tower:
pages 90-107

My
Red Desert:
pages 108-129

My
Thermopolis:
pages 130-155

ACKNOWLEDGEMENTS
Wonderful people contributed to the creation of this book

The first person I would like to thank for making this book a reality is my wife Nancy. She showed great patience with me as we pretty much dedicated the summer of 2012 to this book.

Graphic artist Amy Russian of Lander fulfilled a much larger role than this title implies. She really held the project together.

Pioneer photographer Randy Wagner of Cheyenne was a constant source of encouragement. Former Tourism director Gene Bryan was the first person to encourage me to write this book.

U.S. Sen. Mike Enzi was an early booster of the book and even wrote a chapter. On fishing, naturally. Jim Smail took time out of his busy schedule to take me on field trips to the desert. Our first trip was March 27, 2012. My daughter Shelli Johnson provided much needed advice and wrote the first chapter.

Scott Copeland of Lander came through with more photos than anyone else. He also provided expertise in improving the quality of many of the photos in this book, especially mine.

Pat Schmidt of Thermopolis signed on early to write the chapter about his favorite place but also did much more than that. My old friend

Dean Conger captured this fisheye image of tourists crowded around Morning Glory Pool in Yellowstone 40 years ago.

Clay James was not eager to do the Grand Teton chapter, but I convinced him to do it.

Dewey Vanderhoff of Cody is someone that I have known for 40 years. It was good to work with him again after a long, long time.

Erik Molvar, Laramie, shared with me his experience in producing books of this type. Photographer Dan Hayward of Laramie offered important advice on how to do a pictorial-type book.

What can you say about photographers like Daryl Hunter, Woody Wooden, Tim Doolin, Jeff Vanuga, Ken Driese, Ken Stoecklin, Reid Wolcott, Paul Ng, RJ Pieper, Fred Pflughoft and all the others? They all were willing to let me use their very best photos, which improved the overall quality of this book.

And then there is Dean Conger. Arguably the greatest photographer to ever come from Wyoming, the hardy 85-year-old provided two wonderful fisheye images.

Sara Millhouse, Pat Schmidt and John Brown helped proofread. Tony Bonse helped pre-market the book.

Thanks also to the State Division of Tourism and the State Parks Division.

—Bill Sniffin

About the primary photographers

This book has become so much better because of the participation of 31 wonderful photographers from all over Wyoming.

All photos in this book are the property of the individual photographers and are copyrighted by those individuals. No reproduction in any way is allowed without their permission. These photographers make their livings from the sale of these photos. If you see something you like, please contact the photographer about how you can purchase a print. Here is information about our photographers:

Scott Copeland is from Lander and his web site is www.threedoglight.com. He has been shooting for 20 years and is very serious about capturing the most unique images possible while retaining the most natural of all settings.

Randy Wagner from Cheyenne is the dean of Wyoming photographers. His company is called The Wagner Perspective and his email is rwagnerfoto@optimum.net

Daryl L. Hunter lives in Jackson where he has been shooting landscape and wildlife images since 1986. His website is www.greater-yellowstone.com and he sells gallery prints and stock photography at "The Hole Picture,"www.daryl-hunter.net

Dewey Vanderhoff has lived in Cody his entire life. You can see more of his Planet Cody collection at www.flickr.com/photos/planetcody/

Tim Doolin lives in Sheridan and his photos can be found at www.timdoolinphotography.com

J. L. "Woody" Wooden lives in Wapiti and is a retired professor from Northwest College. More images may be seen at JLWoodyWooden.SmugMug.com

Ken Driese of Laramie is a University of Wyoming lecturer and his photos can be seen at his website is www.kendriesephoto.com.

Ken Stoecklin owns Beartooth Photography in Casper and his work can be found at www.beartoothphotography.net

Dan Hayward of Laramie has been taking photos for 35 years. More info is available at haywardphoto.com.

Dean Conger is a native of Casper and has a long colorful career with National Geographic magazine. He is retired and lives in Durango, CO.

Jeff Vanuga lives in Dubois and more information can be gathered at jeffvanuga.com.

Paul Ng lives in Rock Springs and you can see more of his work at PaulNgPhotography.com.

Reid Wolcott lives in Riverton and his photos can be seen at www.flickr.com/photos/reidsphotography/

RJ Pieper is a native of Rock Springs and more of his photos can be found at www.sweetwaterphotography.com.

Fred Pflughoft lives in Pinedale and has a distinguished history of photography. His work can be seen at many wonderful coffee table books about Wyoming and the Rocky Mountain Region.

Steve Schlager of Casper has been shooting photos for 20 years and his work can be seen at www.wyoscenicphotos.com.

Erik Molvar is from Laramie and has written 15 books. Most recently, he did a coffee table book called The Red Desert.

Michelle Motherway of Lander has been a busy photographer while also getting college degrees and working in the family business. Her email is motherwayphotography@gmail.com

The late **Bobby Model** was from Cody. His photo images can be found at www.m-11.com.

The late **Mike McClure** was a long-time Lander resident. His images can be found in many great books and in some galleries.

Jared Kail lives in Lander, where he operates an internet company.

Jonathan Green lives in Cheyenne and has worked all kinds of media.

Lara Love is an award-winning journalist who works for the Thermopolis Independent Record.

Mike Smith is an award-winning photographer for the Cheyenne Tribune-Eagle.

Rick Carpenter lives in Cheyenne, where he is the award-winning photographer for the Wyoming Department of Transportation.